Violet's Devotional Sketchbook

Lessons Drawn from the Garden

Written by
Wendy Witherow
and Beverly Elliott

MCP
Mission City Press

Franklin, Tennessee

Violet's Devotional Sketchbook—Lessons Drawn from the Garden
© 2007, Mission City Press, Inc. All Rights Reserved. Published by Mission City Press, Inc.

Illustrations:	Kelly Pulley and Molly van Maarth
Typesetting:	BookSetters, Bowling Green, Kentucky
Cover Design:	Richmond & Williams, Nashville, Tennessee
Cover Photography:	Kelly Pulley and Michelle Grisco Photography
Special Thanks to:	Celia van Maarth and Bob Bubnis for their artistic contributions

For more information, write to Mission City Press at 202 Second Avenue South, Franklin, Tennessee 37064, or visit our Web Site at: www.alifeoffaith.com

---

For a FREE catalog call 1-800-840-2641.

Library of Congress Catalog Card Number: 2007905678
Elliott, Beverly and Witherow, Wendy
Violet's Devotional Sketchbook—Lessons Drawn from the Garden
ISBN 13: 978-1-928749-63-9

Printed in the United States of America
1 2 3 4 5 6 7 8 — 12 11 10 09 08 07

Table of Contents

Introduction

ear Friend,

Welcome to my devotional sketchbook! My name is Violet Travilla and I am so happy to introduce you to the fundamentals of art, poetry, and growing toward God through the pages of this activity book. Even though I'm from the 1870s, the virtues of art and faith are timeless—they are what bring us together in this book. You will see that the Scripture, poetry, and inspiring quotes I have gathered for your enjoyment are works that have stood the test of time and that span many centuries.

Art is one of my favorite pursuits. As a young girl I delighted in spending quiet moments on the dock at my family's lake with my sketchbook in hand. God's beautiful creation always inspires my drawings. When I sketch, I often talk to God and wonder in awe at His designs in nature. Through learning and practicing the fundamentals of drawing, my artistic skill has grown. But I have also grown in my relationship with God as I have learned and practiced the fundamentals of faith. I hope to pass along some of my observations and lessons to you!

For instance, as I have learned to "still" myself in order to observe my current subject matter carefully, I have also learned to "still" my heart so that I can incline my thoughts toward our Heavenly Father. In this time of artistic and spiritual stillness, I draw close to God and welcome Him to draw upon the pages of my own heart—even as my pencil glides across a clean, white sheet of paper. I call this "devotional drawing."

I pray that as you learn the fundamentals of art shared in this book and try your hand at drawing, you will also learn to draw close to your Heavenly Father and take His hand into your own. Are you ready to get started?

In Love and Friendship,

Violet

Devotional Drawing

Be still, and know that I am God.
—Psalm 46:10

Be still . . .

In this book I endeavor to teach you basic drawing techniques through lessons "drawn from the garden." The items you will draw are things you would find in or around a garden, but you will also "draw" from truths and lessons found in God's Word and from observing God's creation around you.

Many of the drawings I have chosen are called still life. A still life is an arrangement of inanimate objects, such as fruit, vases, and flowers, that are used for the purpose of painting or drawing. I hope the tools that I have included in this activity book will get you started on a fun-filled journey of becoming an artist. But, the greater objective of this guide reaches far beyond training you to draw—I hope you will grow closer to God and become skilled in the art of "devotional drawing."

As I shared, through your study of drawing, you will develop a very important spiritual discipline. You will learn the art of being still and silent to help you focus on your subject matter. Likewise, you can learn to become "still" before God and to contemplate the many facets of His character and promises. God is the greatest "subject" we could ever aspire to "draw" and "paint" on the canvas of our lives. God is certainly not a "still life," but rather the "Creator of Life" where all inspiration begins and ends.

> ## "Flower in the Crannied Wall"
>
> Flower in the crannied wall,
> I pluck you out of the crannies,
> I hold you here, root and all, in my hand,
> Little flower—but if I could understand
> What you are, root and all, and all in all,
> I should know what God and man is.
>
> –Alfred, Lord Tennyson (1809-1892)

In this place of stillness and meditation on God and His creation, you will find an awakening in your spiritual senses—your spiritual eyes and ears are opened so that you experience God in a deeper way. You become more aware of His presence and therefore enjoy a closer communion with Him—hence "devotional drawing."

. . . and know that I am God . . .

As I have learned from my own studies, artists must know and observe their subject matter closely. If an artist is drawing a bowl of fruit, she will first keenly observe the shading and light, shape and texture, and proportion and perspective before putting pencil to paper. Artists must learn to look past the obvious and to observe the hidden details of their subject matter. When an artist "knows" her subject matter and has studied it closely, she can accurately reproduce the image in her sketchbook. Studying and knowing your subject matter will help you capture tiny nuances and unique details. Your drawing thus becomes an original piece of art.

The same thing happens when you draw close to God. He becomes more vibrant, brilliant, and spectacular as you "observe" Him closely and thoughtfully. You come to "know" God through a relationship with His Son, Jesus Christ, and through the guidance of the Holy Spirit (the Helper), as you study the Bible, spend time in prayer and in worship, and meditate on God's character and promises.

"Be still and know." The more you "know" God, the more your life becomes a grand "reproduction" of His life within you. You become the living, breathing, walking work of art, created by God Himself, for the whole world to see.

If you have not yet begun a relationship with God through His Son, Jesus, please refer to the section called "The Greatest Plan on Earth" in the back of this book. God wants to compose a beautiful painting on the canvas of your heart, and it starts by asking Jesus into your life.

"Listen in Silence If You Would Hear"

Silently the green leaves grow,
In silence falls the soft, white snow;
Silently the flowers bloom,
In silence sunshine fills a room;
Silently bright stars appear,
In silence velvet night draws near;
And silently God enters in
To free a troubled heart from sin.
For God works silently in lives,
And nothing spiritual survives
Amid the din of a noisy street,
Where raucus crowds with hurrying feet
And blinded eyes and deafened ear
Are never privileged to hear
The message God wants to impart
To every troubled, weary heart.
For only in a quiet place
Can man behold God face-to-face!

Be still, and know that I am God.

–Helen Steiner Rice (1900-1981)
Used with permission of The Helen Steiner Rice Foundation, Cincinnati, Ohio.

The Art of Poetry

As much as I love art, I also adore poetry. Art and poetry make a lovely pair, and I hope you will develop a fond appreciation for both as you go through this book. I have scattered fine literary poems and quotes from many centuries to inspire you further as you learn the art of devotional drawing and quiet contemplation. The techniques used in reading and enjoying poetry are similar to those used in drawing—learning to be still, and being thoughtful, patient, and observant.

Poetry, like drawing, is an artistic expression in which the poet is an artist who uses words to paint a picture or image. Through her mastery of words, the poet can make you feel happy, sad, thoughtful, or inspired. Some poems, like some paintings, can be a bit harder to understand and appreciate at first glance. A quiet, reflective, and observant approach is often required to drink in the meaning and inspiration of these more complex types of poems.

Be it drawing, reading or writing poetry, singing, or dancing, the arts can be an expression of pure and impassioned praise and adoration to God—the Creator of all and the Author of all creativity. He is the Artist of Artists, the Poet of Poets, the Singer of Singers, and the Lord of the Dance. Allow your artwork to be an offering of your heartfelt love and devotion to the Lord of all creation. Let the joy of the Lord flow out of you into your drawings. As you sketch and pour out your heart to Him, allow the Lord, in turn, to sketch His love and beauty onto the canvas of your soul.

Drawing Techniques

Tips to Parents:

This book contains drawings that range from beginner level to advanced. You can encourage your young artist to divide the more challenging drawings into at least two sittings to eliminate frustration. She could complete the final line drawing in one sitting and add the shading and texturing in another. If your child is young, she may only be able to sketch up to the final line drawing (which is usually completed by the third or fourth frame). This makes a beautiful drawing in itself. Tracing the finished drawing is also great fun. Monitor her mood as she works. We want to encourage perseverance, but not at the cost of having fun.

Violet's Drawing Tips:

- Drawing can be enjoyed by everyone. It is not just a "natural" ability that you are born with. Anyone, through practice and perseverance, can learn to draw and enjoy drawing.

- There are no "bad" drawings. The true beauty of art is the thrill of creating something unique only to you. This brings me to the next tip.

- Don't expect your drawings to look exactly like mine. Every artist has her own special way of seeing and drawing objects. Leave room for your own personal and distinctive artistic interpretation.

- As with any skill you are trying to master, patience, perseverance, and repetition are a part of the process. Repeat a drawing multiple times and see how your work becomes more polished.

- Last, but most important, have fun! Enjoy releasing your creativity. As you do this, you are actually tapping into God who is the Almighty Creator and giver of all creativity.

☆Overview of the Drawing Instructions:

Your line drawing:

The first couple of frames will involve the process of identifying and sketching the various lines and shapes found in your subject. Every object you look at can be reduced down to very basic lines and shapes: circles, triangles, squares, and ovals (also called an ellipse). With practice, you can develop an eye for looking beyond the details and seeing only the lines and shapes of an object. Once your subject is captured in lines and shapes, you have completed a "line drawing." The sketching lines on your line drawing should be light enough to erase and will serve as a guide for adding shading and texture.

Adding shading and texture:

Adding shading and texture will change your two-dimensional line sketch into a drawing that has form and depth (three dimensional). Attention to these techniques will make your drawing look more lifelike. An artist must develop the skill to see light and shadows in her subject. I will prompt you to look for the light source (where the light is coming from) in your drawings. The lightest areas on your object are facing the light and the shadows will be on the opposite side.

The different techniques for applying shading or texture are mentioned in the definition section that follows. You may wish to experiment with these before you begin to sketch.

In your drawings, you will add your lighter shading first; these are called your mid-tones. To accomplish this, use light pressure on your standard number 2 pencil (HB) while holding it higher up on the shaft, or use a harder graphite pencil, such as an H or 2H pencil.

In your final frame, you will add the darker values. Hint: If you squint your eyes while looking at my final drawing, you can see the range of values (the different shades of grey) more easily. To build up your shading, you can either press harder with your number 2 pencil (HB) while holding it closer to its point, or use a softer graphite pencil (2B or 4B).

Remember to make the changes between values (shades of grey) smooth and flowing. (See graduation technique below.)

Artistic Terms and Techniques:

Shading

Shading refers to the range of various shades of grey between white and black in a drawing; also referred to as "values." Shading is accomplished by capturing light and shadows to give the object form and a three-dimensional look.

Cast Shadows

Cast shadows are shadows that are closest to the object and on the surface where an object sits. The closer the shadows are to the object, the darker they will be, and they will gradually become lighter as they move away from the object.

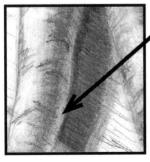

Reflected Light

Reflected light is the faint light created on an object when direct light is reflected or bounced back onto that object from the surface of objects near it. Learning to draw reflected light will give your subject depth and form.

Contour Shading

With this type of shading your lines simply follow the contour or outline of the object. You can use short or long strokes running along the outline of your subject or toward it.

Hatching

This is a series of lines that are drawn closely together and that run in the same direction. They can be long, short, straight, or curved.

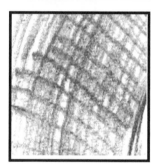

Crosshatching

A series of lines where one set crosses over another set making a woven appearance. These lines can cross at any angle.

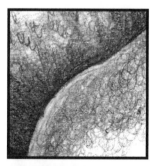

Scribbling

These are a bunch of squiggly, curved lines crossing over each other and going in different directions.

Graduation

This is the term used to describe the smooth and gradual transition from one value to another which creates a more natural look to your drawing. For instance, if you are shading a cast shadow at the bottom of an object, you will start with darker shading and gradually progress into lighter shading.

Highlights

Highlights are the brightest of your light values where the light falls most directly on the object. These areas can be left white or can be lightened by using an eraser.

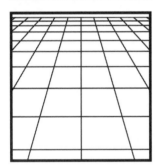

Texture

Texture describes the surface of the object you are drawing. It could be smooth, rough, shiny, dull, furry, hairy, glistening, or jagged. Learning to identify and draw textures will make your picture look more realistic.

Perspective

Perspective is another tool we use to give our two-dimensional drawing a three-dimensional look. Like shading, it helps to give form, shape, and depth to our subject. Simply put, when we use perspective, we are not drawing an image the way it is, but rather, the way we see it from our point of view. For example, a perfectly round plate becomes an ellipse (oval-shape) when it is placed across the table from you.

Below are a few basic perspective principles that we will use in this sketchbook.

1. Objects appear smaller the farther away they are from you. The closer an object is to you, the larger it appears. (Stones on path in garden gate drawing.)

2. Objects in the front of your drawing will overlap objects that are behind them, creating a sense of depth. (Grapes in the fruit drawing, leaves of the daisy drawing.)

3. Lines will begin to grow closer together the further away they travel from you. They will appear the widest apart at the front and sides of an object. (Platter in fruit drawing, rim of birdbath, rim of plate and planks of wood for table in apple drawing.)

4. The closer an object is to you the more detail there is. (Bushes in garden gate drawing.)

5. The front part of a subject is going to appear bigger than the part that is furthest away. A good example of this would be if you found a big mirror and stood sideways, stretching one arm toward it and the other away from it (at an angle where you can still see both hands). Now, look at your reflection as if you were going to draw it. See how big you would have to draw the hand closest to the mirror, and how small you'd have to draw the one that is furthest away? Showing this exaggerated size difference in your art is called "foreshortening."

Materials:

Paper

While you can sketch your drawings on computer paper or any other white paper lying around your house, you may want to purchase an artist's sketchbook. The texture of the paper in a sketchbook is designed to give the best possible end results when drawing with a pencil. Sketchbooks can handle a lot more erasing, are easier to work on, and come in sizes that will give you more room to work with.

Pencils

Graphite pencils are numbered according to the degree of softness of the graphite. The numbers range from 9B, being the softest graphite, to 9H, being the hardest graphite. Softer graphite will leave a darker line and harder graphite will make a lighter line.

B = Black	F = Fine	H = Hard
Softest Graphite (darker lines)		Hardest Graphite (lighter lines)

9B, 8B, 7B, 6B, 5B, 4B, 3B, 2B, B, HB, F, H, 2H, 3H, 4H, 5H, 6H, 7H, 8H, 9H

For most basic drawings you can work between the 2H, HB, 2B, and 4B. Your basic number 2 pencil (HB) will work fine, but you will need to alter the pressure to vary the shading values.

Like the paper, you can use any pencil, but the final drawing can be much improved with a couple of pencils from the art store. They are not too expensive, and these few supplies can really help set the mood as you develop your artistic ability.

Erasers

You may want to use both a vinyl eraser and a kneaded eraser. A vinyl eraser is usually white with a long, rectangular shape. A kneaded eraser is grey and can be molded into different shapes.

The vinyl eraser works well for making patterns and texture by using its edge. If the edge of this eraser gets too dull, you can cut off a new piece using a sharp blade. (Get an adult to help.)

The kneaded eraser works well for lightening larger areas by patting or rubbing your eraser on the paper's surface. This type of eraser is helpful for creating a softer transition between highlights and shadows. For fine, detailed erasing, mold a portion of the eraser into a point. If this eraser becomes dirty, knead it by stretching and reshaping it until it appears clean again.

Pencil Sharpener

There are three basic types of pencil sharpeners: handheld, electric, and crank. Any of these will work fine with graphite pencils.

Drawing: Apple
Lesson: God's Love

Keep me as the apple of your eye; hide me in the shadow of your wings.
—Psalm 17:8

You are the apple of God's eye. Even in a sprawling apple orchard filled with hundreds of apples, He keeps you ever in His sight and cherishes you. He protects you in the shadow of His mighty wings. His intense love is on your side, offering support and guidance in everything you do.

When troubled times come your way, He will shelter you in the quiet shadow of His wings. When doubts linger, find peace by going to the One who holds you in His gaze. When the sun shines warmly upon you, look up and see your Master Gardener smiling down at you.

As you draw these simple, shiny apples, remember how God sees you—as the apple of His eye. Remember that you are important and highly prized by Him. And as you learn this lesson in shading, remember that you can always take refuge in the shadow of God's wings.

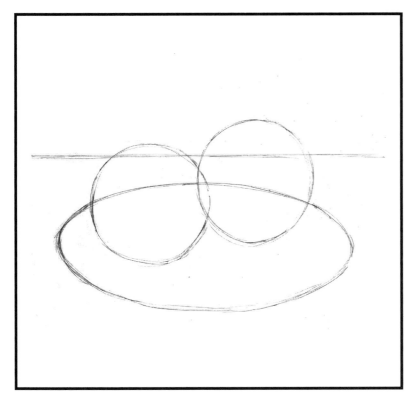

1 Study the completed drawing. Don't the apples look real enough to eat? As your artistic skills grow, your drawings will look more lifelike also. I hope this sketchbook will help get you there. So let's get ready to take our first bite!

It's important to note that every drawing in this book will begin by identifying the basic shapes of our subject matter. In this drawing, there are three basic shapes—two circles (the apples), an oval (the plate), and a straight line (the edge of the table). Position these shapes lightly on your paper so you can easily move things around if you need to erase.

2 When you are happy with the placement of your basic shapes, it's time to start mapping out the details. Because the apple on the left is cut in half, you'll do the same. To do this, draw a diagonal line through the center of the circle, cutting the apple in half. After that, draw an oval shape around the diagonal line within the circle, like I did in my sketch.

3 Staying with the left apple, use the oval you just drew and the diagonal line as guide-marks to draw the curves (resembling the top of a heart). These curves will become the top and bottom of the halved apple.

On the right apple, use gentle, curved lines to draw the dip of the apple and the stem.

Sketch another oval inside the rim of the platter to add more detail. Notice that the top portion of this oval is closer to the edge than the bottom portion. This is how we show perspective.

4 Lightly erase unwanted pencil markings and darken the final sketch lines. Add straight lines for the planks in the table. Pay attention to the angle of these lines to show perspective.

Examine the final drawing to determine where the light source is and then very lightly begin to outline the shape of the "cast shadows" that are under the apples and the platter. Don't miss the curved shadow on the top right of your cut apple.

Go ahead and start adding some of the other details too, like the stem, seeds, and ridge toward the middle of the platter. You have now finished what we call the final line drawing.

5 In order to add depth and form to your drawing, you must think more about shadows and shading. To do this, you need to study the finished drawing very closely to determine where the source of light is coming from. In this case, the light source is the sun, which is behind and to the right of the apples, so all of the shadows need to move the opposite direction. Just as light scatters the darkness in the Bible, think of shadows as darkness that run away from the light! Also, when drawing in shadows, your pencil strokes should follow the "grain" or shape of the object you are drawing (contour shading). Always begin your shading with light pencil strokes and leave areas of highlight (where the light falls most directly) unshaded.

To add texture to your apple, let your pencil strokes follow the grain of the apple skin, fanning out from the stem.

6. The last step is the final shading in which you darken all of the places where the shadows are the deepest. This will make the highlights pop out and give your drawing the appearance of life.

Here's a trick to help you see more clearly where your light and dark areas are (values): Squint at the final drawing. This eliminates distracting detail and helps you visualize your shadowed areas.

Press heavier with the pencil toward the center of the apple where the stem meets the core, and also darken the lip of the plate. To brighten up your highlights, use your eraser to show where the sun is reflecting off of the apple on the right.

Now step back and enjoy your creation! Even as you delight in your apple sketch, remember that you are God's beautiful creation—the apple of His eye. He delights in you!

A WORD APTLY SPOKEN IS LIKE APPLES OF GOLD IN SETTINGS OF SILVER.

—PROVERBS 25:11

"Under His Wings"

Under His wings I am safely abiding,
Tho the night deepens and tempests are wild;
Still I can trust Him—I know He will keep me,
He has redeemed me and I am His child.

Under His wings, what a refuge in sorrow!
How the heart yearningly turns to His rest!
Often when earth has no balm for my healing,
There I find comfort and there I am blest.

Under His wings, O what precious enjoyment!
There will I hide till life's trials are o'er;
Sheltered, protected, no evil can harm me,
Resting in Jesus I'm safe evermore.

Under His wings, under His wings,
Who from His love can sever?
Under His wings, my soul shall abide,
Safely abide forever.

–William O. Cushing (1823-1902)

A SEED HIDDEN IN THE HEART OF

AN APPLE IS AN ORCHARD

INVISIBLE.

—A WELSH PROVERB

Excerpt taken from
"The Lotos-Eaters"

Lo! sweeten'd with the summer light,
The full-juiced apple, waxing over-mellow,
Drops in a silent autumn night.
All its allotted length of days
The flower ripens in its place,
Ripens and fades,
and falls, and hath no toil,
Fast-rooted in the fruitful soil.

–Alfred, Lord Tennyson (1809-1892)

WE ARE BORN BELIEVING.
A MAN BEARS BELIEFS,
AS A TREE BEARS APPLES.

—RALPH WALDO EMERSON (1803-1882)

Drawing: Bird
Lesson: God's Loving Presence

Are not two sparrows sold for a penny? Yet not one of them will fall to the ground apart from the will of your Father. And even the very hairs of your head are all numbered. So don't be afraid; you are worth more than many sparrows.

—Matthew 10:29-31

The next time you are sitting quietly in your garden or on your patio, take time to consider the birds, as Jesus encouraged. They have much to teach you about trusting your Heavenly Father.

God is mindful of all of His creation. He knows where the sparrow builds her nest to birth her young. His presence is there. His presence is there as she finds her food and as she soars the heavens with freedom and purpose. He knows when this same sparrow breathes her last breath and returns to the dust of the earth. His presence is there also.

If the simple sparrow has captured God's watchful gaze, then how much more are His loving eyes always on you? His gaze is so fixed on you, His presence so surrounding you, that He is aware of every single strand of hair on your head! If you can grasp this wonderful truth, you will enjoy a life of trust and peace—free from fear and worry—just like those feathered friends. You, too, shall rise up on wings of faith and sing your Maker's praise.

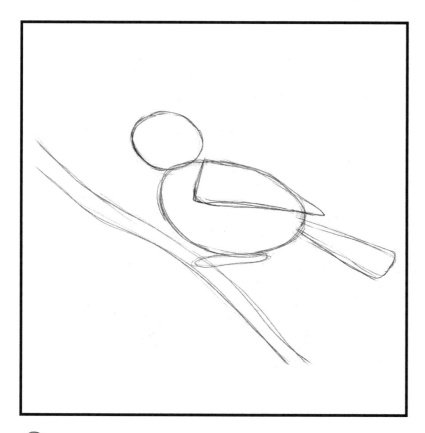

1 Let's focus our eyes on the details of this little feathered fellow, and our drawing skills will soar to new heights.

When drawing animals, it's not always easy to see the basic shapes. For me, it is easier to try to visualize the shape of the bird without the feathers. First, draw an oval for the head and a larger oval for the body. Be careful to position the head in the right spot over the body, and make sure the head is not too big or too small. Next, rough out the shape of the wing, leg, tail, and branch.

2 I always like to sketch the eyes first, since this is where our attention is first drawn. Note that the circle for the eye is off-center a bit, because the bird is looking toward us a little.

With that in mind, position the beak of the bird a little further into the circle as well.

Now we'll lightly draw in the patterns of the markings and colors of the bird. The throat and underside are lighter. There is also a section in the middle of the wing where there is a row of lighter-colored feathers.

3 As we start to define the features a little more, we can focus on the way the feathers lie over the shapes we drew earlier.

Take a close look at the original drawing and study the details.

Notice the way the bird's head is somewhat flat on top and how it connects to the body without much of a neck. Erase the unwanted lines now, and start to concentrate on the shape of the wings, the joint of the leg, and the nails on its little claws.

Give the bird just a touch of a smile as you define the beak, and you've completed the line drawing.

4 It will take different shades of grey to give the bird its distinctive patterns.

I like to start with the eyes and draw in highlights. Rather than coloring the eye solid black, give your bird a spark of life by adding reflective light points. It might look a little funny at first, but the closer your drawing gets to the final stage, the more life-like it will be because of this added touch.

Don't forget to leave the highlight on the beak.

5 As you add in the different shades of grey, make short, light strokes with your pencil. Don't sharpen your pencil to too much of a point, as you want to give this bird a soft look. Make sure that your strokes follow the contour of the bird's body.

Look at the patterns of light and dark on the final drawing, which suggest the bird's varied coloring. Work on the medium and light tones first, gradually building up to the dark places.

Don't forget the smooth bark of the branch. Notice how I have highlights under the branch that get darker as they move to the edge. This gives a cylindrical appearance.

"OVERHEARD IN AN ORCHARD"

SAID THE ROBIN TO THE SPARROW, "I SHOULD REALLY LIKE TO KNOW ...

WHY THESE ANXIOUS HUMAN BEINGS RUSH ABOUT AND WORRY SO?!"

SAID THE SPARROW TO THE ROBIN, "FRIEND, I THINK THAT IT MUST BE,

THAT THEY HAVE NO HEAVENLY FATHER, SUCH AS CARES FOR YOU AND ME."

—ELIZABETH CHENEY (CIRCA 1859)

Keep deepening your shadows. By now it should appear that this feathered friend has its eye on you! Clean up with an eraser, and the little bird should look like it is ready to spring into flight any second.

Whenever you feel down, look up and find a bird in the sky and be reminded that your Heavenly Father is watching after you.

LOOK AT THE BIRDS OF THE AIR; THEY DO NOT SOW OR REAP OR STORE AWAY IN BARNS,
AND YET YOUR HEAVENLY FATHER FEEDS THEM.
ARE YOU NOT MUCH MORE VALUABLE THAN THEY?
—MATTHEW 6:26

"His Eye Is on the Sparrow"

Why should I feel discouraged, why should the shadows come,
Why should my heart be lonely, and long for heaven and home,
When Jesus is my portion? My constant friend is He:
His eye is on the sparrow, and I know He watches me;
His eye is on the sparrow, and I know He watches me.

Refrain
I sing because I'm happy,
I sing because I'm free,
For His eye is on the sparrow,
And I know He watches me.

"Let not your heart be troubled," His tender word I hear,
And resting on His goodness, I lose my doubts and fears;
Though by the path He leadeth, but one step I may see;
His eye is on the sparrow, and I know He watches me;
His eye is on the sparrow, and I know He watches me.

Refrain
Whenever I am tempted, whenever clouds arise,
When songs give place to sighing, when hope within me dies,
I draw the closer to Him, from care He sets me free;
His eye is on the sparrow, and I know He watches me;
His eye is on the sparrow, and I know He watches me.

Refrain
–Civilla D. Martin (1866-1948)

EVEN THE SPARROW HAS FOUND A HOME, AND THE SWALLOW A NEST FOR HERSELF, WHERE SHE MAY HAVE HER YOUNG—A PLACE NEAR YOUR ALTAR, O LORD ALMIGHTY, MY KING AND MY GOD.
—PSALM 84:3

"Upon the Swallow"

This pretty bird, oh, how she flies and sings!
But could she do so if she had not wings?
Her wings bespeak my faith,
her songs my peace;
When I believe and sing, my doubtings cease.
–Robert Herrick (1591-1674)

IN ALMOST EVERYTHING THAT TOUCHES OUR EVERYDAY LIFE ON EARTH, GOD IS PLEASED WHEN WE'RE PLEASED. HE WILLS THAT WE BE AS FREE AS BIRDS TO SOAR AND SING OUR MAKER'S PRAISE WITHOUT ANXIETY.
—A.W. TOZER (1897-1963)

USE TALENTS YOU POSSESS; THE WOODS WOULD BE VERY SILENT IF NO BIRDS SANG THERE EXCEPT THOSE THAT SANG BEST.
—HENRY VAN DYKE (1852-1933)

YOU ARE TO ME, O LORD,
WHAT WINGS ARE
TO THE FLYING BIRD.
—ANONYMOUS

Drawing: Tree
Lesson: Strength and Endurance

... They will be called oaks of righteousness,
a planting of the LORD for the display of his splendor.
— Isaiah 61:3

A tree completes any garden by providing shade, shelter, and beauty for all who recline beneath it. In the Bible, God says that His people will grow to become like strong, enduring trees. As you draw this tree, imagine yourself growing a tall, strong trunk with leafy branches. Imagine your roots going deep and wide in the knowledge of God's great love for you. This is who you are as a child of God. Take possession of His promise and plant yourself firmly in Christ.

Prayer: Lord, make my life like a grand old oak tree—able to withstand the storms of life which come my way, while my arms never cease to be lifted in humble acceptance and praise. Teach me to allow the mighty winds of adversity to make me strong and stable, rooted in Your love, so that I can become a place of refuge and refreshment for those who have become wearied along the way.

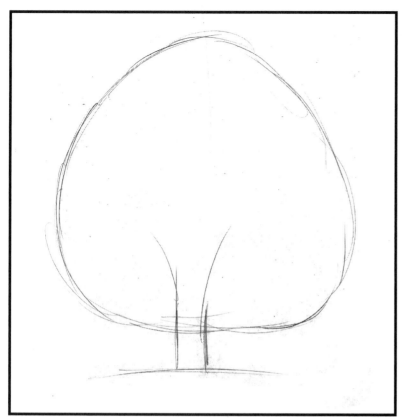

1 Let's unlock the mystery of how to draw a magnificent tree with full, healthy branches and a delightful, dangling swing. As always, we'll start by sketching the basic shapes. Notice that the main body of the tree is in the shape of a teardrop. The trunk is drawn up into the teardrop shape. A line at the bottom indicates the ground.

2 Before moving on, pause for a moment to study the finished drawing. Notice that the leaves are in groups. In this step you will draw the shapes of those groupings, just as I've done in the example to the right.

When you have finished this, you can start drawing in the branches, connecting each grouping to the trunk.

3 Now add definition to the leaf groupings. Notice that you don't need to draw individual leaves, but rather, jagged lines that give the impression of leaves. Allow your pencil to squiggle away freely. Imagine the shape of a leaf as you work.

Next, go back to the branches. It's time to sketch them in a little darker. Let the branches cross over each other as they raise their leaves toward Heaven.

Finally, begin a light sketching of the root at the base of the tree. Notice that it faces toward you. Erase all unwanted lines and then move on to the next step.

4 For this next step, you need to consider the light source so that you know where to place the shadows. Look at the final drawing to determine the direction of the sun. Can you tell that the sun is above and to the right of the tree?

Carefully begin shading in the spaces between the leaf groupings. This will add more depth to your tree. Use scribble and/or hatching lines to add texture and shading to the leaf groupings. All the while, remember that where the sun is shining directly on a grouping, you should leave it lighter. Concentrate your shading toward the bottom left.

As you add texture to the branches and trunk, use shorter strokes to give it the look of bark.

Finally, use short, random strokes to "grow" some grass. Let the grass come toward you a bit.

5 Now it's time for some detailed shading. Try squinting at my finished tree to see the values (shades of grey) come alive. The branches that are deeper in the tree need to be darker, as they are getting more shade. The outer branches that are exposed to more light should be darker on the bottom with some highlights on top. You can use your eraser now and then to show spots of light on the trunk and branches where the sun makes it past the leaves.

For your final touch, draw in the swing.

Now you have a wonderful reminder of how strong and beautiful your life can become as you remain rooted in Christ.

"A Prayer"

Teach me, Father, how to go
Softly as the grasses grow;
Hush my soul to meet the shock
Of the wild world as a rock;
But my spirit, propt with power,
Make as simple as a flower.
Let the dry heart fill its cup,
Like a poppy looking up;
Let life lightly wear her crown
Like a poppy looking down,
When its heart is filled with dew,
And its life begins anew.

Teach me, Father, how to be
Kind and patient as a tree.
Joyfully the crickets croon
Under shady oak at noon;
Beetle, on his mission bent,
Tarries in that cooling tent.
Let me, also, cheer a spot,
Hidden field or garden grot—
Place where passing souls can rest
On the way and be their best.

–Edwin Markham (1852-1940)

~~~

GOOD TIMBER DOES NOT GROW WITH
EASE; THE STRONGER THE WIND,
THE STRONGER THE TREES.
—J. WILLARD MARRIOTT (1900-1985)

WHY ARE THERE TREES I NEVER WALK
UNDER BUT LARGE AND MELODIOUS
THOUGHTS DESCEND UPON ME?
—EXCERPT FROM SONG OF THE OPEN
ROAD BY WALT WHITMAN (1819-1892)

~~~

THE WONDER IS THAT WE CAN SEE THESE
TREES AND NOT WONDER MORE.
—RALPH WALDO EMERSON (1803-1882)

~~~

"Trees"

I think that I shall never see
A poem lovely as a tree.

A tree whose hungry mouth is prest
Against the sweet earth's flowing breast;

A tree that looks at God all day,
And lifts her leafy arms to pray;

A tree that may in summer wear
A nest of robins in her hair;

Upon whose bosom snow has lain;
Who intimately lives with rain.

Poems are made by fools like me,
But only God can make a tree.

–Joyce Kilmer (1886-1918)

Drawing: Daisies
Lesson: God's Glory in Creation

The heavens declare the glory of God;
the skies proclaim the work of his hands.

—Psalm 19:1

Nature is speaking a language of its own—not audible words, but a spiritual language you hear with your heart. All of nature speaks of God's glorious handiwork. From the stars in the sky and the flowers in a field to the plantings in a garden, all speak of God's power and majesty.

Psalm 19 says that the heavens, as all of nature, proclaim to the earth the glorious power and awesome majesty of God. Likewise, Psalm 148 speaks of the stars praising God in the heavens. Daisies, our "earthly stars" (as the poets say), also join in this divine testimony of the magnificent handiwork of God.

As you draw the dainty petals of these starry flowers plucked from the garden, allow your heart to be touched by their story of the unfailing, faithful love of your awesome Creator. Look for God's faithful love in every blade of grass and in every flower's face.

1 Before we begin, let's become very still and focus intently on the beautiful details that God has drawn into these daisies. Drawing these cheerful flowers will be a fun task.

As with all of our pictures, we will start by observing the shapes of our subject matter. Look at the final drawing and focus on the center of the flowers. Notice that they are not a perfect circle like they would be if we were looking at them straight on. We have to make them oval shaped because we are seeing them from an angle. The more sideways they appear, the flatter the ovals. Copy what I'm doing and you'll see what I mean as we go.

Draw the bigger ovals first—they will determine the size and placement of the flowers' faces.

After the bigger ovals are drawn, draw in the smaller ovals. Then draw in the stems. The stems should flow out of the center of the smaller ovals.

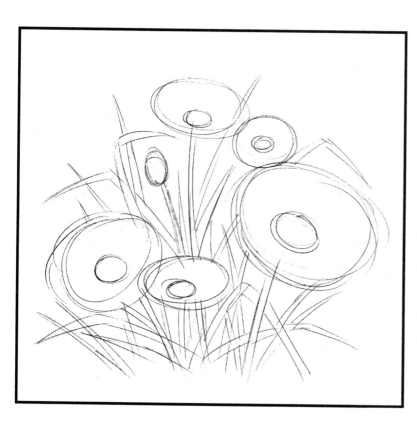

2 Next, begin to lay out the random way the leaves and the grass mix in with the flowers. Don't get frustrated here. Remember, yours doesn't have to look just like mine.

When you draw the blades of grass, let a few of them bend and cross over other blades of grass. Don't forget to sketch lightly.

3 Once you have mapped out the drawing, it's time to sharpen your pencil (if you need to) and begin adding the details. Draw in the petals—feel free to be original. A daisy has petals that are very fragile, like tissue. They bend easily, but that is part of what makes them look beautiful.

Use your eraser to define which blades, stems, and petals are in the foreground and background. Also erase any other unwanted lines. Darken final sketch lines.

NEVER LOSE AN OPPORTUNITY OF SEEING ANYTHING THAT IS BEAUTIFUL;
FOR BEAUTY IS GOD'S HANDWRITING—A WAYSIDE SACRAMENT.
WELCOME IT IN EVERY FAIR FACE, IN EVERY FAIR SKY, IN EVERY FAIR FLOWER,
AND THANK GOD FOR IT AS A CUP OF BLESSING.
—RALPH WALDO EMERSON (1803-1882)

4 With all of the planning done, it's time to apply texture and shading to your drawing. To do this, we must identify the light source. In this picture, the sun is above and to the right. As you draw, imagine the light coming from that direction. This will help you figure out where your shadows need to be.

While adding shadows, let your pencil strokes follow the "grain" or shape of the object. In this case, the shadows on the petals need to travel the length of the petals. You can shade in the undersides of the blades of grass and leaves now, too. Don't forget to work lightly at first. You will darken the shading in the next step.

Add the bumpy texture to the center of the flowers.

5 You are getting close now! Look closely at the center of the flowers again. Where the shadow is, I put the bumpy scribbles closer together and even on top of each other. As I got closer to the light source, I used them less and spread them further apart. You might want to practice this on another piece of paper first.

This drawing is really shaping up and is already good enough to sign and give to a friend, but there is one last thing you can do to give your drawing that finished look.

The last step is the final shading. This is where you commit to the lines you've drawn by making the deepest parts of the shadow a little darker. This will take your art from a flat sketch to a pencil drawing that has depth and dimension. For highlight effects, lightly shade some areas of the stems; where the light is strongest, leave the area unshaded.

That should be it! Great job! The next time you see a patch of carefree daisies blooming for all to enjoy, remember that those little "stars" declare God's artistic grandeur. What an amazing artist our God truly is!

"Daisy Time"

See, the grass is full of stars,
Fallen in their brightness;
Hearts they have of shining gold,
Rays of shining whiteness.

Buttercups have honeyed hearts,
Bees they love the clover,
But I love the daisies' dance
All the meadow over.

Blow, O blow, you happy winds,
Singing summer's praises,
Up the field and down the field
A-dancing with the daisies.

—Marjorie Lowry Christie Pickthall (1883-1922)

Excerpt taken from "Flowers"

Wondrous truths, and manifold as wondrous,
God hath written in those stars above;
But not less in the bright flowerets under us
Stands the revelation of his love.

Bright and glorious is that revelation,
Written all over this great world of ours;
Making evident our own creation,
In these stars of earth, these golden flowers.

—Henry Wadsworth Longfellow (1807-1882)

PRAISE HIM, SUN AND MOON,

PRAISE HIM, ALL YOU SHINING STARS.

PRAISE HIM, YOU HIGHEST HEAVENS

AND YOU WATERS ABOVE THE SKIES.

LET THEM PRAISE THE NAME OF THE LORD,

FOR HE COMMANDED

AND THEY WERE CREATED.

—PSALM 148:3-5

"Where Innocent Bright-Eyed Daisies Are"

Where innocent bright-eyed daisies are,
With blades of grass between,
Each daisy stands up like a star,
Out of a sky of green.

—Christina Rossetti (1830-1894)

Drawing: Butterfly

Lesson: Freedom in Christ

So if the Son sets you free, you will be free indeed.

—John 8:36

Where there are flowers, there are butterflies. The poet Robert Frost calls them "flowers that fly." Butterflies flitter around the bushes, blending their gorgeous colors in with those of your garden. As you sketch this beautiful "flying flower," may it remind you of freedom.

In Christ you are as free and beautiful as this butterfly. Through the sacrifice of His life, you are now free from the bonds of sin and death. This butterfly was once confined to a cocoon, but now it has risen in glorious splendor! So have you been set free to display Christ's beauty in the earth. Give thanks for this wonderful freedom—and fly, little flying flower, fly!

1 This Peacock butterfly is flaunting his uniquely patterned wings for you to draw and admire. Let's get started before he flies away!

Begin by looking over my finished drawing so that you can plan your composition. Put pencil to paper and begin to rough out the basic shapes of all of the elements.

2 Now that the shapes are in place, begin to sketch in the contours of the wings, the shape of the body, and the antennae on his head.

Each flower is at a different angle, so as you sketch the directions of the petals, be mindful of the position of each flower. The one at the far right is the flattest, so the petals fan out accordingly. The flower on the left is straight on, so each petal fans out evenly. These are important details to consider as you plot out the flowers because they will give your drawing real depth.

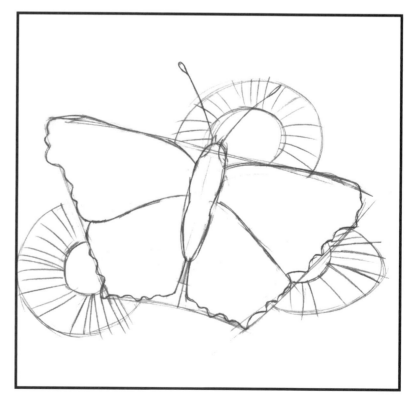

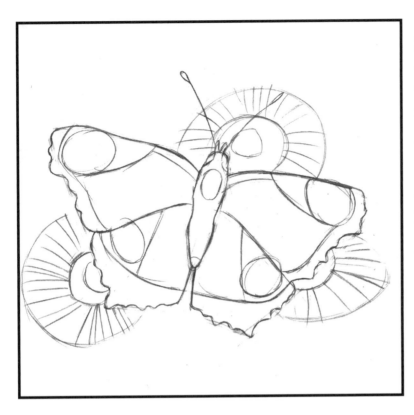

3 Next, begin to lay out the shapes of the markings on the wings and body. I've drawn these in just a little darker as a guide for you. You'll want to keep your lines light, especially as you build your confidence as an artist.

God has fashioned each delicate wing like a fragile flower petal decorated with matching designs. Let's see if you can make the wing designs match also.

4 As you refine the drawing, work on the shapes within the shapes in the wing patterns. You'll need a sharp pencil to get these details right—and some patience.

Consider the flowers next. The beauty of the petals lies in their irregularities and frailty. Some petals are bent, some broken, some short, and some long, but they will all come together to form something beautiful.

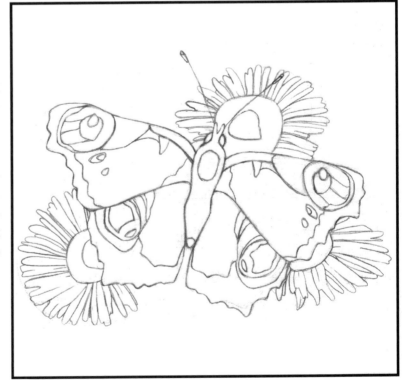

5 Now it is time to work on the shading. Because of the felt-like nature of the wings, start with the light and medium tones. Build up the shading, especially next to the body on the lower two wings. Now add detail to the center of the daisies and work on the flower details, too.

Next, use a small pencil eraser (or an eraser that you can sharpen) to clean up the white parts of the round designs on the wings. Clean up around the wings also, as this won't be as easy to do once you get to your final stages.

Once this is done, go back in with the pencil for the detail work. Take advantage of the natural dullness of your pencil. As it gets duller, it becomes better suited for certain areas of your drawing. When you have to re-sharpen, go back to the fine lines you need to work on.

Because of the symmetry of the wings, as you do one detail, go to the same spot and work up that same detail on the other wing. This will keep the pencil sharpness, shading, and style consistent on both wings.

Go over the drawing again with a sharp pencil to do the last of the detail work. Use the scribbling technique to add texture to the center of the flowers. You'll notice that I didn't spend much time on the daisy petals. Adding too much detail in the background can distract people from what we really want them to see. In this case, our fanciful butterfly is the main attraction.

What I want you to see now is that God is capable of transforming you in the most remarkable and miraculous ways. He desires for you to soar on the heights of His freedom. Allow the love of God to change you from the inside out, and always remember that you are free, indeed!

"Eutopia"

There is a garden where lilies
And roses are side by side;

And all day between them in silence
The silken butterflies glide.

I may not enter the garden,
Though I know the road thereto;

And morn by morn to the gateway
I see the children go.

They bring back light on their faces;
But they cannot bring back to me

What the lilies say to the roses,
Or the songs of the butterflies be.

—Francis Turner Palgrave (1788-1861)

HAPPINESS IS A BUTTERFLY, WHICH WHEN
PURSUED, IS ALWAYS JUST BEYOND YOUR
GRASP, BUT WHICH, IF YOU WILL SIT DOWN
QUIETLY, MAY ALIGHT UPON YOU.
—NATHANIEL HAWTHORNE (1804-1864)

"Blue-Butterfly Day"

It is blue-butterfly day here in spring,
And with these sky-flakes down in flurry on flurry
There is more unmixed color on the wing
Than flowers will show for days unless they hurry.

But these are flowers that fly and all but sing:
And now from having ridden out desire
They lie closed over in the wind and cling
Where wheels have freshly sliced the April mire.

—Robert Frost (1874-1963)

Excerpt taken from
"To a Butterfly"

I've watched you now a full half-hour,
Self-poised upon that yellow flower;
And, little Butterfly! indeed
I know not if you sleep or feed.
How motionless!— not frozen seas
More motionless! and then
What joy awaits you, when the breeze
Hath found you out among the trees,
And calls you forth again!

—William Wordsworth (1770-1850)

Drawing: Daffodils
Lesson: Joyfulness

Let the fields be jubilant, and everything in them.
Then all the trees of the forest will sing for joy.
—Psalm 96:12

Poets and artists observe nature from a very unique and refreshing perspective. For instance, the writer of Psalm 96 saw the trees as "singing for joy" at the coming of the Lord. William Wordsworth, in his poem "Daffodils," described the flowers as "fluttering and dancing in the breeze." The reader is left with a delightful impression of the writer's own artistic expression.

When you study garden scenes for your own drawing or poem, try to be like a poet and see the "joyful dance" going on around you. Imagine the branches of a willow tree "slowly swaying" peacefully in a summer breeze or a wayfaring cloud waving a jubilant "bon voyage" as it travels across the sky and onward to Heaven. Look for joy and life in the scenery around you, and then express that joyfulness in your art.

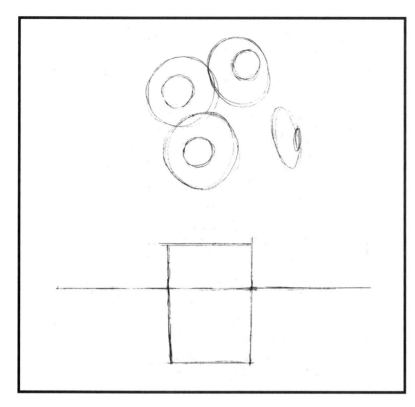

1 This lesson is about joy, so as you create your drawing, infuse each line with the joy you feel in your heart. Are you short on joy? Lift a prayer to Heaven and ask God to fill you with the joy of His presence! Are you ready to have some fun?

As always, start by sketching the basic shapes.

The horizon line will become the edge of the table. Whenever you draw a horizon line, it's best not to draw it in the middle of your paper, as this gives the illusion of cutting your drawing in half. When you are laying out a drawing, put that line in either the upper third or lower third of the page, as shown.

2 This drawing is a little tricky, so while I'll tell you what I'm doing, the best thing to do is look at my example and imitate what I do.

Lightly sketch the ovals for the top and bottom of the crock using the top and bottom lines of your rectangle as the center for these ovals. Draw the oval at the top smaller than the one at the bottom.

Focus now on the neck of the crock. Lightly sketch the second oval lower and equal distance from the first. Add your connecting lines and let them flow into the sides of your crock.

Now it's time to put the flowers in the crock, so add in the stems and leaves.

3 With everything nicely placed, you can work on the details.

Have fun with the flowers by adding a very small dot in the center of the three larger circles. Draw six ovals for the petals of each flower extending between the dots and the inside edge of the big circle.

Observe the flower on the far right. Because we are looking at it from the side, the center of the flower appears cone shaped and the petals are narrow teardrop shaped.

Finally, for the rim of the crock, sketch a smaller oval just inside of the top oval before moving on to the next step.

4 It's time to get out your eraser and rid your picture of unwanted lines. Erase the outer circles you used as guides for the petals. To make the center of your flowers, erase the lines inside the smaller center circles.

Next, notice how the petals of the daffodils overlap. Erase unwanted lines from inside every other petal to make them appear as if they are in front of the other petals. Add a point to each petal to make it teardrop shaped.

At the center of the flowers are what appear to be little stems. Add them in now.

Lightly sketch the outline of the cast shadow at the bottom right of your crock.

Next, darken final sketch lines and add detail to the flowers, stems, and leaves.

5 Now you'll add texture and shading to the drawing. Notice that the texture of the crock is splotchy. We can achieve this look by using the scribbling technique. By varying the pressure of the pencil, we can attain the different levels of darkness. To give the crock that glazed effect you can use your finger to smooth and blend these different shades together, but be careful not to smudge the rest of the drawing.

The leaves have dark stripes in them and the centers of the flowers have a ruffle which you can darken now. Add texture to your flower petals using your hatching technique. The closer together your lines are, the darker the appearance.

Remember the light source as you are doing this. With the light in front and to the left, the shadow has to run away from you to the right. The shadow should be darker toward the base of the crock, getting lighter as it fades into the distance. Take your time during this stage.

AND 'TIS MY FAITH, THAT EVERY FLOWER ENJOYS THE AIR IT BREATHES.
—WILLIAM WORDSWORTH (1770-1850)

You are just about finished. Squint at my final drawing to locate the dark and light values more easily. Add the final shading, texture, and detail by either using a softer lead pencil or by drawing harder. Continue with the hatching technique for the flowers and the scribbling technique for the crock.

For the final touch, use the eraser to touch up the highlights and to clean up any unwanted lines and smudges.

That's it! You're finished. Now you can share your joy-filled drawing with others. Maybe you'll even see a sparkle of joy in their eyes as they behold your artful masterpiece!

"Daffodils"

I wander'd lonely as a cloud
That floats on high o'er vales and hills,
When all at once I saw a crowd,
A host, of golden daffodils;
Beside the lake, beneath the trees,
Fluttering and dancing in the breeze.

Continuous as the stars that shine
And twinkle on the Milky Way,
They stretch'd in never-ending line
Along the margin of a bay:
Ten thousand saw I at a glance,
Tossing their heads in sprightly dance.

The waves beside them danced; but they
Out-did the sparkling waves in glee:
A poet could not but be gay,
In such a jocund company:
I gazed – and gazed – but little thought
What wealth the show to me had brought:

For oft, when on my couch I lie
In vacant or in pensive mood,
They flash upon that inward eye
Which is the bliss of solitude;
And then my heart with pleasure fills,
And dances with the daffodils.

–William Wordsworth (1770-1850)

~~

THE EARTH LAUGHS IN FLOWERS.
—RALPH WALDO EMERSON (1803-1882)

"Buttercups"

Like showers of gold dust on the marsh,
Or an inverted sky,
The buttercups are dancing now
Where silver brooks run by.
Bright, bright,
As fallen flakes of light,
They nod
In time to every breeze
That chases shadows swiftly lost
Amid those grassy seas.
See, what a golden frenzy flies
Through the light-hearted flowers!
In mimic fear they flutter now;
Each fairy blossom cowers.
Then up, then up,
Each shakes its yellow cup
And nods
In careless grace once more –
A very flood of sunshine seems
Across the marsh to pour.

–L.M. Montgomery (1874-1942)

~~

"Legend of the Daffodils"

Each time a Guardian Angel
notices a good deed–
a prayer, kindness or sacrifice–
she plucks a gold star from the heavens
and sends it to earth,
where it blooms as a golden daffodil.

–Author Unknown

Drawing: Fruit

Lesson: Fruit of God's Spirit

But the fruit of the Spirit is love, joy, peace, patience, kindness, goodness, faithfulness, gentleness and self-control. Against such things there is no law.
—Galatians 5:22-23

The natural result of Christ's life growing in our hearts is producing the life-changing "fruit of the Spirit" as listed in Galatians 5:22-23. As the life of Christ flows through us, we become like trees whose strong, spreading branches are laden with the ripe, luscious fruit of love, joy, peace, patience, kindness, goodness, faithfulness, gentleness, and self-control. As that fruit grows and ripens in our lives, a wonderful thing happens! Our Master Gardener will use that Spirit-grown fruit to nourish and bless all who should wander into our orchards.

As you draw this still life of delicious garden fruit, remember that the fruit of the Spirit is growing in your very own heart. Look for ways you can share that fruit with others, and always remember to stay connected to the Vine—our Lord Jesus Christ.

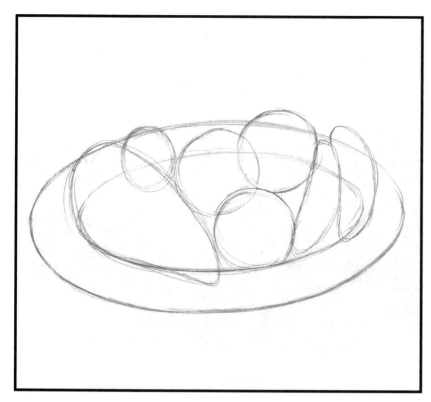

1 As you try your hand at this advanced drawing, resist the urge to become discouraged or to give up. As you face this challenge (and all of life's challenges), nurture the fruit of the Spirit in your life, such as patience and faithfulness. These character-building qualities will give you the perseverance you need to stay the course!

Let's get started. As you draw the shapes, many will overlap. It's important to draw the whole shape, even if part of it will be hidden by another piece of fruit. This helps you to create a more realistic look for your fruit and to place each piece properly.

2 Once you have all of the shapes placed nicely together, it's time to include the individual features of each shape, such as elongated tops on your lemon and pear and placement of stems.

Now sketch in the grapes. Make sure that they overlap and that they vary slightly in size—just like in real life. Work in the stem running through the grapes.

3 Continue to add detail to your fruit and to erase all unwanted lines. Use your eraser to make some grapes fully shaped. Allow other grapes to be overlapped. This creates an illusion of depth and realness.

Now turn your attention to the platter. To simplify this drawing, you can leave the platter in this oval shape. But if you're up to the challenge, lightly sketch the lip of the platter, first pointing out, then in.

This brings us to a great example of perspective. Notice how the closer the platter is to you, the more space there is between these points in the lip. As the points get further away from you, however, the space between each point gets closer (perspective).

Once again, erase unwanted sketch lines from the edge of the platter and darken all final sketch lines.

4 This probably seems like a big jump from the previous step, but it really isn't. It demonstrates the transformation that happens to your line drawing when you add shading and texture. In this picture the sun is positioned above us, behind us, and to our left. This means that the shadows will be more intense on the right. Notice how the shadow follows the inside lip of the platter. On the left side of the platter the shadow is darkest on the inside of the lip, but as the platter curves toward us, the light begins to strike the inside of the lip, creating a highlight.

Use your scribbling technique for shading and for adding texture to the pear, banana, lemon, and grapes. The hatching technique works well for the apples. Leave highlights unshaded.

5 Finally you're at the point where you can get darker with the pencil and really work on the details. By squinting at this frame, you can see more easily where the darkest and lightest shades are which will help you add your shadows and highlights. Sharpen your pencil to a fine point to work the fine lines of the grapes and the stems. I change the areas I'm shading as my pencil gets dull. I will start with the stems, but as the pencil wears, I might move to the shadows underneath the platter. When the pencil is really dull, I'll work on some of the softer shading on the banana, pear, or edge of the platter.

If you have a kneaded eraser, you can use it on the pear and banana to create a softer transition from your shadows to highlights. A vinyl eraser works best for the grapes since that shading requires a harder, more defined contrast.

Now you can stand back and enjoy the "fruit" of your labor! Perseverance, especially in challenges, can bring forth very satisfying results.

Excerpt taken from
"Odyssey"

Close to the Gates a spacious Garden lies,
From the Storms defended and inclement Skies;
Four Acres was the allotted Space of Ground,
Fenc'd with a green Enclosure all around.
Tall thriving Trees confessed the fruitful Mold:
The reddening Apple ripens here to Gold,
Here the blue Fig with luscious Juice overflows,
With deeper Red the full Pomegranate glows,
The Branch here bends beneath the weighty Pear,
and verdant Olives flourish round the Year.

—Homer, circa 850 B.C.

DO NOT BE AFRAID TO GO OUT ON A LIMB...
THAT'S WHERE THE FRUIT IS.
—H. JACKSON BROWN, JR.

A TREE IS KNOWN BY ITS FRUIT; A MAN BY HIS
DEEDS. A GOOD DEED IS NEVER LOST;
HE WHO SOWS COURTESY REAPS FRIENDSHIP, AND
HE WHO PLANTS KINDNESS GATHERS LOVE.
—BASIL (329-379)

LOVE IS A FRUIT IN SEASON AT ALL TIMES, AND
WITHIN REACH OF EVERY HAND.
—MOTHER TERESA (1910-1997)

Excerpt taken from
"The Apple Tree"

When an apple tree is ready
for the world to come and eat,
There isn't any structure
in the land that's "got it beat."
There's nothing man has builded
with the beauty or the charm
That can touch the simple grandeur
of the monarch of the farm.
There's never any picture
from a human being's brush
That has ever caught the redness
of a single apple's blush.

There's the promise of the apples,
red and gleaming in the sun,
Like the medals worn by mortals
as rewards for labors done;
And the big arms stretched wide open,
with a welcome warm and true
In a way that sets you thinking
it's intended just for you.
There is nothing with a beauty
so entrancing, so complete,
As an apple tree that's ready
for the world to come and eat.

—Edgar A. Guest (1881-1959)

Drawing: Birdbath

Lesson: Rest and Reflection

He leads me beside quiet waters, he restores my soul.
—Psalm 23:2-3

A birdbath is a cheery feature in any backyard or garden. There's something delightful about watching a bird take a drink or splash joyfully in the still water. Like a bird, we can also "drink" and "bathe" in the still, healing waters of God's presence.

As you draw this birdbath, let it be a reminder to *rest* and *reflect* upon God's goodness. Set aside time each day to read a verse of Scripture and reflect upon its meaning, or simply quiet your thoughts and pray. Either way, take a few minutes to look deeply into God's eyes and refresh yourself in the peace He gives. Are you troubled? Bathe in the healing waters. Are you joyful? Plunge in and splash with glee! Drink deeply in His presence. Let Him *restore* your soul.

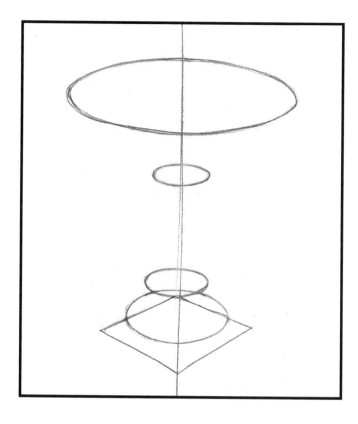

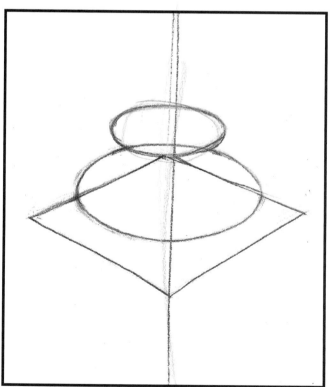

1 Let's quietly reflect upon the symmetry and precision of this elegant garden birdbath before we begin.

In its simplest form, the birdbath drawing is a series of ovals that are centered and stacked upon each other with a diamond-shaped base.

Start by sketching a vertical line down the center of your page. You will use the vertical line to center and line up all of your shapes. Next, draw the diamond-shaped base, as shown in the close-up picture. See how our square looks more like a diamond shape? This is because we are seeing it at an angle (perspective). Center the two bottom ovals on top of the diamond-shaped base.

Next, draw the top two ovals, being careful to keep them centered on the vertical line.

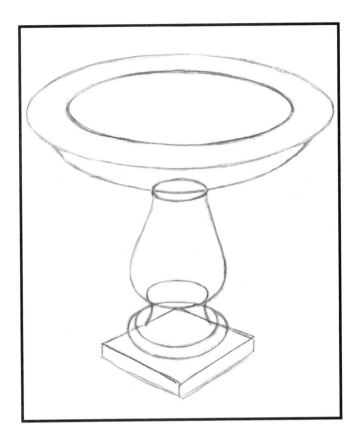

2 To create the rim of the birdbath, add a larger oval around the top oval. The rim of the basin should be drawn so that it is narrower at the back of the basin than the front and sides (perspective).

Now draw in the lines to form the basin, pedestal, and stand as shown in the example.

In order to check your drawing to make sure it's even on each side (symmetrical), try this little trick: hold your drawing up to a mirror and view it in the reflection to see if any parts are off balance.

3 Erase unnecessary lines from the sketch. Draw in the leaves that are sculpted on the pedestal. To simplify the drawing, you can omit the leaves.

Add a waterline to the basin and draw in the reflection of the trees in the water. You may want to refer to the final drawing to help with the reflection. Feel free to use originality as you draw in the reflection.

reflected
light

4 Our light source is coming from behind the birdbath, so the shadows will point toward us. Add shading to the trees reflected in the water.

In addition to the light that is coming through the trees, there is a secondary light source created by the sun as it reflects off of other objects. In this case, sunlight is bouncing off of the ground and brightening the underside of the birdbath. Look at the final drawing to see how this reflected light softly illuminates the underside of the basin and the sculpted leaves.

This reflected light also helps us define features with shadow that couldn't be done any other way. If you look at the bottom arrow, you'll see how the darker shading meets the diffused light, to define that feature.

COME TO ME, ALL YOU WHO ARE WEARY AND BURDENED, AND I WILL GIVE YOU REST.
—MATTHEW 11:28

5 With one last trip over the drawing with your pencil to define details and deepen shadows, you will see a birdbath that birds would come from miles around to enjoy.

Still water in a stone basin—
A Pool of Reflection
A Place of Refreshment
A Promise of Rest

"I Heard the Voice of Jesus Say"

I heard the voice of Jesus say, "Come unto Me and rest;
Lay down, thou weary one, lay down Thy head upon My breast."
I came to Jesus as I was, weary and worn and sad;
I found in Him a resting place, and He has made me glad.

I heard the voice of Jesus say, "Behold, I freely give
The living water; thirsty one, stoop down, and drink, and live."
I came to Jesus, and I drank of that life giving stream;
My thirst was quenched, my soul revived, and now I live in Him.

I heard the voice of Jesus say, "I am this dark world's Light;
Look unto Me, thy morn shall rise, and all thy day be bright."
I looked to Jesus, and I found in Him my Star, my Sun;
And in that light of life I'll walk, till traveling days are done.

–Horatius Bonar (1808-1889)

BE AT REST ONCE MORE, O MY SOUL, FOR THE LORD HAS BEEN GOOD TO YOU.
—PSALM 116:7

"Come, Rest Awhile"

Come, rest awhile, and let us idly stray
In glimmering valleys, cool and far away.

Come from the greedy mart, the troubled street,
And listen to the music, faint and sweet,

That echoes ever to a listening ear,
Unheard by those who will not pause to hear–

The wayward chimes of memory's pensive bells,
Wind-blown o'er misty hills and curtained dells.

One step aside and dewy buds unclose
The sweetness of the violet and the rose;

Song and romance still linger in the green,
Emblossomed ways by you so seldom seen,

And near at hand, would you but see them, lie
All lovely things beloved in days gone by.

You have forgotten what it is to smile
In your too busy life–come, rest awhile.

–L.M. Montgomery (1874-1942)

Drawing: Roses
Lesson: Innocence and Purity

*But thanks be to God, who always leads us in triumphal procession
in Christ and through us spreads everywhere the fragrance
of the knowledge of him.*

—2 Corinthians 2:14

In the language of flowers, the rose speaks of love and beauty and the rosebud is the symbol of beauty and youth.

In your girlhood, you are God's beautiful rosebud—a testament of purity, innocence, and love designed for the pure joy of your Master Gardener. Each day your delicate petals are slowly and gently opening up to the love and wonder of your Master Gardener. Each day you become a little more fragrant as you grow toward the One who loves you so. Cling to your purity and innocence. Rest assured that someday, under your Master Gardener's loving care, you will burst into glorious bloom. You will grow into an exquisite, mature rose planted in this world to represent His beauty and to release the aromatic fragrance of His love to all you meet.

1 This drawing will offer a healthy challenge to a budding artist. Take your time and do your best to capture the innocence and breathtaking loveliness of these gorgeous flowers.

Let's begin by outlining the basic, simple shapes. A circle represents the outside of the rose's edge and an oval will be the rosebud. We will also add smaller ovals to represent the centers of the flowers. The petals of our lovely roses fan out from the center, and that's where we'll begin our sketch also. Our drawing will "bloom" from there.

2 You may want to study my final drawing to see how the petals are going to fall. Starting with the very center of each bud, carefully begin to copy the shape of each petal. Go lightly and work in a relaxed, loose manner. Don't be dismayed if your petals aren't exactly like mine. Let your rose take on a beauty of its own. Take your time and enjoy the process.

3 After you are done lightly planning out the positioning of the petals, it's time to get serious with your pencil and begin to define the outline of each one.

When you are finished with the petals, do the same thing with the leaves. Finally, clean up unwanted lines with your eraser.

4 Now it's time to stop and consider the light source of this picture. Look closely at the final drawing. Notice that each petal is opening to catch the light in its own unique way.

Let's look close-up at the shading of the smaller rose on the left. See how the darker shading on the rose petals appears deeper and closer to the stem? The darker you shade an object the further or deeper in the background it appears; highlights bring the object forward and upward. This helps to create the illusion of dimension and depth.

5 You will use this same shading technique with the big rose. Again, note how the shading of one petal makes the edge of the next petal stand out. You'll want to get darker where each petal connects to the stem.

As you work on your shading, consider the direction of your lines. If you look closely, you'll see that the lines should follow the curves that go around the bud or the curves that come out from the bud.

6 Crosshatching is a great technique that works really well when drawing roses. Notice how I crossed the lines following around the bud with the lines coming out from the bud.

Crosshatch closely together in the darker areas of the petals and spread it out (to make it look lighter) in the highlighted areas of the petals.

You may want to practice crosshatching on a separate piece of paper before you apply it to your roses.

7 You are almost finished. To polish your drawing, darken the darkest areas and use your eraser to touch up highlights and clean up where needed.

Step back and admire your lovely roses. These roses will always be in bloom on your paper. And you will always be in bloom under the Master Gardener's care!

JOYFUL, JOYFUL, WE ADORE THEE, GOD OF GLORY, LORD OF LOVE;
HEARTS UNFOLD LIKE FLOWERS BEFORE THEE, OPENING TO THE SUN ABOVE.

EXCERPT TAKEN FROM "JOYFUL, JOYFUL, WE ADORE THEE"
—LYRICS BY HENRY J. VAN DYKE (1852-1933)

66

"Roses"

I went to gather roses and twine them in a ring,
For I would make a posy, a posy for the King.
I got an hundred roses, the loveliest there be,
From the white rose vine and the pink rose bush and from the red rose tree.
But when I took my posy and laid it at His feet
I found He had His roses a million times more sweet.
There was a scarlet blossom upon each foot and hand,
And a great pink rose bloomed from His side for the healing of the land.
Now of this fair and awful King there is this marvel told,
That He wears a crown of linked thorns instead of one of gold.
Where there are thorns are roses, and I saw a line of red,
A little wreath of roses around His radiant head.
A red rose is His Sacred Heart, a white rose is His face,
And His breath has turned the barren world to a rich and flowery place.
He is the Rose of Sharon, His gardener am I,
And I shall drink His fragrance in Heaven when I die.

–Joyce Kilmer (1886-1918)

"Roses"

You love the roses–so do I. I wish
The sky would rain down roses, as they rain
From off the shaken bush. Why will it not?
Then all the valley would be pink and white
And soft to tread on. They would fall as light
As feathers, smelling sweet; and it would be
Like sleeping and like waking, all at once!

–George Eliot,
pen name of Mary Ann Evans (1819-1880)

WHICH IS LOVELIEST IN A ROSE? ITS COY BEAUTY WHEN IT'S BUDDING, OR ITS SPLENDOR WHEN IT BLOWS?
—GEORGE BARLOW (1847-1914)

WE CAN COMPLAIN BECAUSE ROSE BUSHES HAVE THORNS, OR REJOICE BECAUSE THORN BUSHES HAVE ROSES.
—ABRAHAM LINCOLN (1809-1865)

Drawing: Garden Gate

Lesson: Fellowship with God

As God has said: "I will live with them and walk among them,
and I will be their God, and they will be my people."

—2 Corinthians 6:16

Just as there are physical gardens where tranquility and peace hang like the branches on a tree, so there is such a garden within your heart, a spiritual retreat, where you can meet with your Lord and find rest for your weary soul.

God walks in the garden of your heart; He is always waiting for you there. Will you take time out from the clamor and busyness of your day to meet with the Gardener of your soul? The gate to this garden of communion is always open!

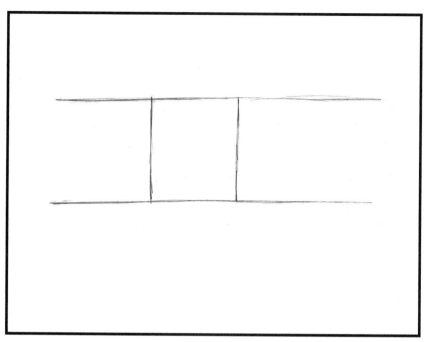

1 At first glance this drawing might look difficult to reproduce, but it's actually going to be a fast and fun walk in the park.

As you look over the drawing on the opposite page, you'll see that all of the shading is achieved by using quick, long strokes with each series going in different directions and using different shades. This particular shading technique helps to keep the focus on the most important part of the drawing—the path and the gate.

As a general rule, when drawing landscapes, it is a good idea to position the main horizon line a bit off-center. This makes the picture more pleasing to the eye. In this case, if you imagine the halfway point on the paper, you'll see that I've placed the bottom edge of the gate just below that line.

The gate doesn't need to be centered either. Place it a little further to the left to allow room for the placement of the dense foliage on the right.

2 Next you can quickly outline the path, the tree, and each of the bushes. Remember to sketch lightly.

Working quickly with your strokes will give this drawing the feeling of spontaneity and the appearance of wild, natural growth that happens when God sets life in motion.

3 Once the basic layout is done, it's time to refine just a little bit. Erase the lines that are not needed and add in branches, the trees in the background behind the gate, and the stones on the path. As the path winds toward the gate, we need to remember that each stone needs to get narrower, both horizontally and vertically (perspective). Since the sizes of the stones are irregular, there is no set formula to use for placement. Just make it pleasing to the eyes.

4 Outline the trees and bushes to give them that leafy look. Be confident and carefree, and at the same time make each line count because you won't be going over these again. On the trees in the background, make your squiggly leaf lines smaller and closer together. As you do trees and bushes that are closer in, make them a little bigger.

Now you'll need to work on the fence by installing the hinges and putting up the boards. Lightly pencil these in, taking care to make them as even as you can. When you draw cityscapes or houses, rulers come in handy, but for this, let's draw them by hand to give them more of a weathered look.

5 Because the focal point of the drawing is going to be the gate, you really need to concentrate your efforts on getting it the way you want it before all of the shading starts on the foliage.

Go over your board lines and make the individual corner cuts on the top of each board. By the time you are done, the only thing you should have left to do on the fence should be the shading.

6 With the layout now behind us, it is time to work on the shading. To get started on this phase you need to be loose and free. Make room on your desk so that you can turn your paper at the correct angle for each section you focus on. A long pencil might help, as you don't want the palm of your hand to rest on anything you've already worked on.

Practice the quick side-to-side stroke on a piece of scrap paper and find the angle that is most comfortable to you. It looks hard, but it really gets easier with practice.

When you master this technique, go back to your drawing, turn the paper to get the correct angle, and start shading the trees in the distant background. Apply different shading values and change the direction of pencil strokes to show contrast between these trees and the other foliage in this picture. This keeps each plant separate from the next and adds depth to the drawing.

Remember, work quickly and have fun.

7 Continue the same shading technique to finish the rest of the trees and bushes.

To give the bushes in the foreground a little more detail and form, slightly change the direction of the shading lines on the same bush.

For every drawing that you create, try to add an extra touch that will make your picture special and unique. With the birdbath it is the reflection of the trees on the water. In the bird drawing it is the light in his eyes. In this case it is the shadow going across the pathway.

As you shade in the stones, notice that some stones have sunlight on them and others are in the shade. The stones that are in the sunlight should be a little darker than the grass around them. Leave the stones in the shade alone so they can appear lighter.

8 Once you've given each plant its own individual shading, it's time to add more detail, shadow, and texture to give the plants form and dimension.

Draw in some new leaf lines that follow the form of the bush. Add shading to these new lines by using the crosshatching technique. This crosshatching of lines will make the leaves stand out.

9 Now turn your attention to the fence. Add vertical grain to the wood, following the length of the boards. Work on fine detailing the hardware on the fence.

10 ✩ To finish this drawing, stand back and squint at my final picture in order to see the darkest values. Deepen the shadows for extra emphasis. If you have extra art pencils with different darkness levels, try them out here.

Your garden gate is now finished. Does it beckon you to come and fling it open? Do you wonder what delights God has waiting for you within? You can open the gate right now by simply opening your heart to the Master Gardener and enjoying sweet fellowship with Him.

"My Garden"

A garden is a lovesome thing, God wot!
Rose plot,
Fringed pool,
Ferned grot—
The veriest school
Of peace; and yet the fool
Contends that God is not—
Not God! In gardens! When the eve is cool?
Nay, but I have a sign;
'Tis very sure God walks in mine.

−T.E. Brown (1830-1897)

~

MY SOUL FINDS REST IN GOD ALONE.
—PSALM 62:1

~

"My Garden of Prayer"

My garden beautifies my yard
And adds fragrance to the air,
But it is also my cathedral
And my quiet place of prayer,
So little do we realize
That the glory and the power
Of He who made the universe
Lies hidden in a flower.

−Helen Steiner Rice (1900-1981)

Used with permission of The Helen Steiner Rice Foundation,
Cincinnati, Ohio.

"In an Old Town Garden"

Shut from the clamor of the street
By an old wall with lichen grown,
It holds apart from jar and fret
A peace and beauty all its own.

The freshness of the springtime rains
And dews of morning linger here;
It holds the glow of summer noons
And ripest twilights of the year.

Above its bloom the evening stars
Look down at closing of the day,
And in its sweet and shady walks
Winds spent with roaming love to stray,

Upgathering to themselves the breath
Of wide-blown roses white and red,
The spice of musk and lavender
Along its winding alleys shed.

Outside are shadeless, troubled streets
And souls that quest for gold and gain,
Lips that have long forgot to smile
And hearts that burn and ache with pain.

But here is all the sweet of dreams,
The grace of prayer, the boon of rest,
The spirit of old songs and loves
Dwells in this garden blossom-blest.

Here would I linger for a space,
And walk herein with memory;
The world will pass me as it may
And hope will minister to me.

−L.M. Montgomery (1874-1942)

Drawing: Bunny

Lesson: God's Goodness in Creation

*For every animal of the forest is mine, and the cattle on a
thousand hills. I know every bird in the mountains, and the
creatures of the field are mine.*

—Psalm 50:10-11

⭐ One of the enjoyments of planting a garden is sharing it with others–both people and animals. Your garden will become a banqueting table for some furry critters. Welcomed or not, these cute, little thieves will silently sneak in and leisurely dine on your tender lettuces, radishes, and carrots. The bunny has an amazing ability to sit as silent and still as a statue, taking in his surroundings with big, dark eyes and fun, flickering ears. His cute little wiggly nose and white cottony tail make you wish you could scoop him up and cuddle him closely.

As you draw this sweet garden bunny, thank God for all of the wonderful creatures He has made for your enjoyment. God delights in all of His creation and His goodness is over all.

1 Our furry friend is sitting perfectly still as if he is posing for his portrait. But quick as a flash he'll be hopping right off the page to dine in a nearby garden.

As always, you'll need to "see through" this little fellow and break down his body into shapes that you can arrange on your paper.

2 Next you can focus on the eyes, then the nose, and ears and paws last. Take care with the placement of these features.

3 Begin working on the shape of the eye, the contour of his face, and the way the ears connect to his head. Start out light so you can erase if you need to. When your composition looks similar to mine, you can commit to stronger lines.

As you look at the eye, draw the bottom eyelid, the corners, and the points of reflective light in its pupil, which will give the bunny a spark of life.

Don't forget to erase the unwanted lines and then add in the whiskers.

4 This probably seems like a big jump from the last step, but rabbits are known for big jumps! Actually, drawing in the fur is not hard. See how all the fur is drawn in short strokes, basically following the shape of the rabbit's body. This gives it that soft and cuddly look. Do these hairs

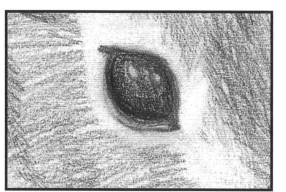

lightly. Later you'll add darker hair to give it that wild rabbit look.

The light source is in front of the rabbit, so the ears are casting a shadow across its back. This lighting also helps us define some areas with shadows, such as the jaw line, the legs, and the backside where the

5 Now go over the fur coat with some darker strokes, as I've done here. Make them even darker where there are shadows. When you are finished, space out some additional hairs that are darker yet.

Next, put in a shadow underneath the little critter so that he has something to stand on.

Use an eraser to create the effect of soft white fur, gently lifting some of the shading off of the bottom of his paws, as well as the jawline and tail. The kneaded eraser works best for this. After that, you should be done!

When you look at God's creation through your artistic eyes, you'll get to know God even better. He is the greatest artist of all, but His art isn't confined to a sheet of paper—it moves, breathes, hops, nibbles, and twitches its nose!

1 The flowers and leaves in this drawing have beautiful curves and twists, giving them an almost lifelike quality. When you are finished with this one, you'll be quite pleased!

Let's begin by putting the basic shapes of the composition in place.

2 With pen and ink, or watercolors, once you've made a line, you are pretty much stuck with it. With graphite pencils, however, you can keep erasing and redrawing until you are satisfied with what you see. Just remember to sketch lightly. This reminds me of the grace of God. No matter what mistakes we make, He can make us white as snow if we ask Him to.

We will now begin to draw in the beginnings of the lines that will become the leaves, flowers, and stems. Using the small circles at the center of your flowers for starting points, lightly draw your five petals extending out to the larger circle. Give your stems that carefree twist and turn which are characteristic to violets, and have fun with those big heart-shaped leaves.

3 With drawing we build on the lines and shapes we've done along the way, so let's do that now, paying close attention to detail added to the flowers, stems, and leaves. Erase unwanted sketch lines. At this point in my drawing I began to add in rocks. It may be difficult to sketch the shape of the rocks as I have drawn them. Your rocks can be any shape or size that you choose. To simplify this drawing, you can omit the rocks altogether. Darken your final sketch lines and get ready for the fun part—shading.

ONE OF THE MOST ATTRACTIVE THINGS ABOUT THE FLOWERS
IS THEIR BEAUTIFUL RESERVE.
—HENRY DAVID THOREAU (1817-1862)

4 Now it's time for shading. The light source is coming from the above right. Let the direction of the shading follow the direction of the leaves. The leaves have deep creases, so get darker inside of the grooves. Leave the highlighted areas of the leaves unshaded.

Let the thicker hatching lines for shading and texture radiate out from the center of the flowers. Add final detail to the center of the flowers. Now we're almost there.

5 We'll finish up by getting dark with our pencil again, giving this violet a dramatic and beautiful look. Squint at the final picture to locate your values (dark and light areas) more easily.

Add all of the cast shadows that the leaves are leaving behind on the rocks. Go lighter with all of your shading and your lines on the stones, mostly to keep from distracting from the flowers.

Are you happy with your drawing? If not, keep practicing. Your skills will improve. But most importantly, take a lesson from the lovely violets. Allow your heart to be content and joyous with your abilities as they stand right now.

"The Violet"

Down in a green and shady bed
A modest violet grew;
Its stalk was bent, it hung its head,
As if to hide from view.

And yet it was a lovely flower,
Its colour bright and fair;
It might have graced a rosy bower,
Instead of hiding there.

Yet there it was content to bloom,
In modest tints arrayed;
And there diffused its sweet perfume,
Within the silent shade.

Then let me to the valley go
This pretty flower to see;
That I may also learn to grow
In sweet humility.

—Jane Taylor (1783-1824)

"A Child's Prayer"

God, make my life a little light
Within the world to glow;
A little flame that burneth bright
Wherever I may go.
God, make my life a little flower
That giveth joy to all,
Content to bloom in native bower,
Although the place be small.
God, make my life a little song
That comforteth the sad,
That helpeth others to be strong
And makes the singer glad.
God, make my life a little staff
Whereon the weak may rest,
And so what health and strength I have
May serve my neighbors best.
God, make my life a little hymn
Of tenderness and praise;
Of faith, that never waxeth dim,
In all His wondrous ways.

—M. Betham-Edwards (1836-1919)

O wind, where have you been,
That you blow so sweet?
Among the violets
Which blossom at your feet.

The honeysuckle waits
For Summer and for heat
But violets in the chilly Spring
Make the turf so sweet.

— Christina G. Rossetti (1830-1894)

87

Drawing: Vegetables
Lesson: Seeing God in Simple Things

O Lord, how many are Your works! In wisdom You have made them all; the earth is full of Your possessions.

—Psalm 104:24 (NASB)

Artists must train their eyes to see detail and design in the objects they are drawing. We, too, can train our eyes to look deeply and intently at details in the world around us—details easily missed by the casual glance. A stroll through any garden will reveal thousands of beautiful details.

There is beauty in everything God has made. Psalm 104:24 testifies that the earth is full of God's handiwork and wisdom. Open your eyes to appreciate and notice the wondrous miracle in God's world. Look with wonder and expectation at that which seems common. Be careful that you are not so easily "wowed" by the glamorous and grandiose that you miss the treasures hidden in simpler things. The little things are the most easily missed, and yet oftentimes they have the most to say!

As you draw this still life of vegetables gathered from the garden, focus on the smallest details of each individual item. Craft each line with an eye toward the details. As you study and draw the world through the lens of a sharp, artistic eye, you will begin to experience a whole new understanding of how big and magnificent God really is!

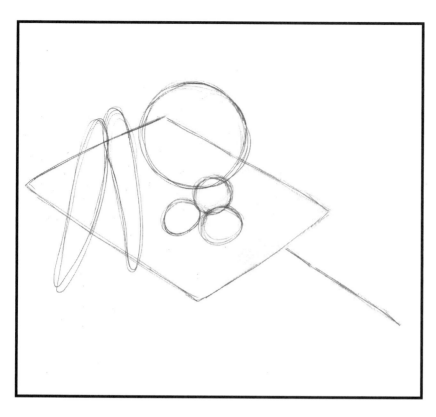

1 This advanced drawing will challenge not only your skills as an artist, but also your ability to focus on and capture details. So take your time and enjoy the process of growing as an artist.

In this drawing you will work with many different textures and shapes, such as the grain of the wood, the random folds of the radish leaves, the way a cast shadow falls off of a surface, and the textures of different kinds of vegetables.

We'll focus on other details, too, like the veins in the leaves, the hair-like roots of the radishes, the shine of the bell pepper, and the knot in the leather strap used to hang the cutting board.

Begin by mapping out the basic shapes of the vegetables and the cutting board, and add a light guideline, as shown, to place the handle.

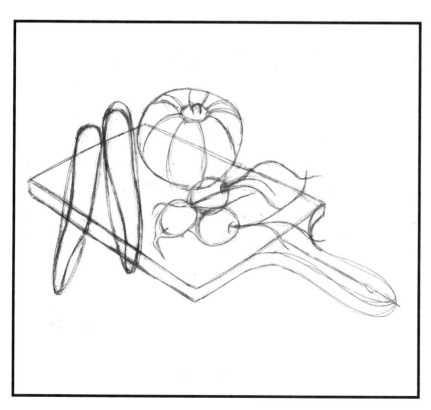

2 After sketching the basic shapes you'll add the thickness of the board along with the handle. Add the creases in the bell pepper, the beginning of leaves of the radishes, the odd shapes of the carrots, and the elongated radishes.

3 Now you can erase all unwanted sketch lines before moving on. In keeping with our lesson's theme of focusing on the details, keep refining your shapes into more detailed versions of each object. The rough edges of the leaves, the fine lines of the roots, the twist of the leather strap, the hard ridges of the bell pepper, and the softer ridges of the carrots are all features you'll need to include.

As you sketch the leaves and the gently curving stems of the radishes, work lightly and in a relaxed and free manner. Don't get bogged down with making the leaves look exactly like mine.

Remember to start out light and then get darker. If you start out too dark, repeated eraser use will begin to change the texture of the paper and cause some unwanted effects.

4 Next you can work with shadows and highlights to give the drawing form and depth. As you can see, the light is coming from the left. You also have some reflected light on the back of the vegetables.

With the carrots, imagine the angle and get the pencil shading to follow that cylindrical shape. As their shadows fall against the wooden cutting board, shade in the direction of the grain. In the same way, follow the shape of your bell pepper with your pencil strokes. Because the bell pepper is smoother, you'll need the more dramatic highlights that you get from using a vinyl eraser. The carrot and radish highlights can be accomplished by adjusting pressure on your pencil. Leave brightest highlights white.

Finally, notice the way the shadows of the carrots drop off of the cutting board. You have a slight cast shadow in front of your cutting board. These are the details that make all the difference.

5 Squint at my finished picture to visualize the range of values (dark and light shades). Along with the final shading, you'll also add in the fine lines that make up the veins of the leaves, the grain of the wood (be careful to let it drop off of the edge as it comes to the end of the board), and that extra bit of shadow coming off of the end of the carrot to the far left. Let that fade out as the light diffuses it. Brighten highlights with an eraser.

There is such a thing as over-working a drawing, but in this case, I think it's a good idea to study each object in your drawing and compare it to the final drawing so you don't miss anything.

Focus in and observe closely. You may even see some details that I have missed.

As you study your drawing, rest assured that even beyond the details you do see, God has been at work, creating and recreating, building and forming, and using all of the little things to declare His great majesty.

"For Little Things"

Last night I looked across the hills
And through an arch of darkling pine
Low-swung against a limpid west
I saw a young moon shine.

And as I gazed there blew a wind,
Loosed where the sylvan shadows stir,
Bringing delight to soul and sense
The breath of dying fir.

This morn I saw a dancing host
Of poppies in a garden way,
And straight my heart was mirth-possessed
And I was glad as they.

I heard a song across the sea
As sweet and faint as echoes are,
And glimpsed a poignant happiness
No care of earth might mar.

Dear God, our life is beautiful
In every splendid gift it brings,
But most I thank Thee humbly for
The joy of little things.

–L.M. Montgomery (1874-1942)
Excerpt taken from "To See a World"

To see a World in a Grain of Sand
And a Heaven in a Wild Flower
Hold Infinity in the palm of your hand
And Eternity in an hour . . .

–William Blake (1757-1827)

BEHIND EVERY FLOWER STANDS GOD.
—JAPANESE PROVERB

EVERY DEWDROP AND RAINDROP HAD A
WHOLE HEAVEN WITHIN IT.
—HENRY WADSWORTH LONGFELLOW
(1807-1882)

THE INVARIABLE MARK OF WISDOM IS TO
SEE THE MIRACULOUS IN THE COMMON.
—RALPH WALDO EMERSON (1803-1882)

Drawing: Watering Can
Lesson: Useful Vessels

Now in a great house there are not only vessels of gold and silver but also of wood and clay, some for honorable use, some for dishonorable. Therefore, if anyone cleanses himself from what is dishonorable, he will be a vessel for honorable use, set apart as holy, useful to the master of the house, ready for every good work.
—2 Timothy 2:20-21 (English Standard Version)

In this lesson we are drawing a garden vessel—the watering can. The garden shed is full of other vessels, such as clay pots, glass jars, and plastic pitchers. Each has a specific purpose that is useful to the gardener and beneficial to the growth and health of the garden.

Believe it or not, you are an important "vessel" useful to the Master Gardener. He invites you to carry His life into the great harvest fields of the earth—the people who have not yet heard the message of Jesus' love and forgiveness. Sometimes you may carry living water—like this watering can—that pours out the love of Christ on a dry, thirsty land to encourage and refresh those who are struggling. Other times you may be as a flowerpot strategically placed by the Master Gardener to bloom and release the fragrance of His hope and joy to those around you.

In this season of your life, what are you carrying and dispensing among God's harvest fields? As you draw this watering can, pause to consider what kind of vessel you are in God's Kingdom. What is His purpose for you?

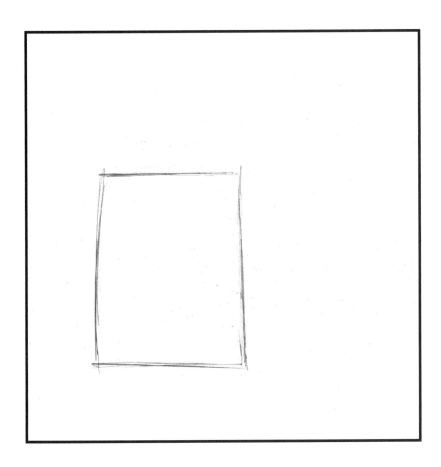

1 To begin this drawing, you will simply sketch a rectangle that approximates the shape of the can. The top and bottom lines of the rectangle will be the center points of our oval.

Symbolically, this rectangle could represent what life may have been like for you without Christ—a box, closed off on all sides. In a short time though, this box will transform into a watering can that can be filled and refilled with living waters.

2 In this step we'll sketch the ovals for the top and bottom of the can, using our horizontal lines as center markers.

Study my final version and then lightly sketch in the handles and the spout until you have everything pretty close to where it should be.

3 Begin this step by erasing the unwanted lines.

When drawing man-made objects, try to be precise with your lines. Take your time as you define the various characteristics of the watering can.

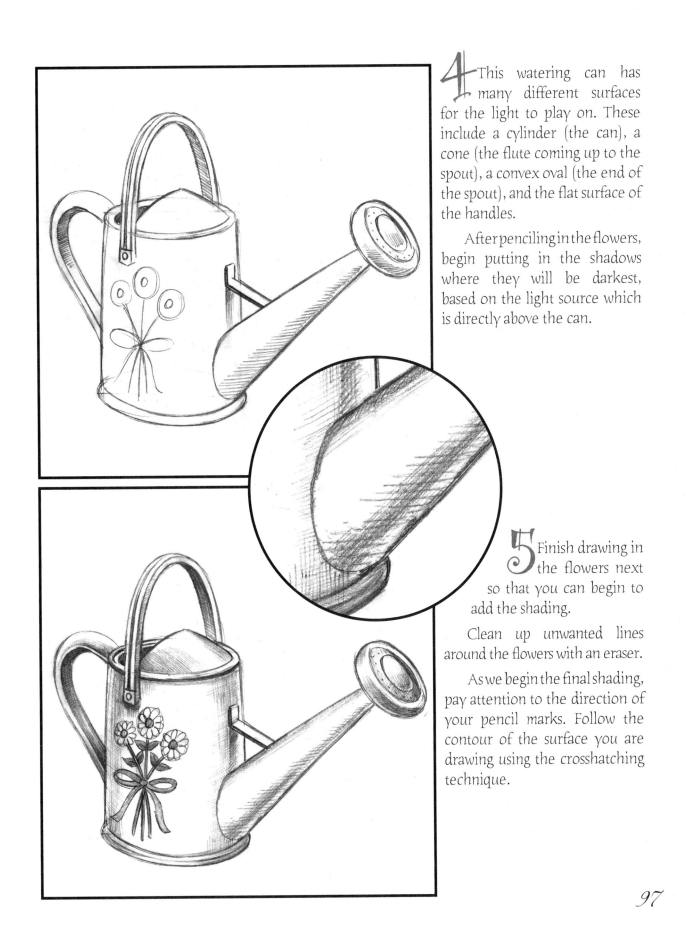

4 This watering can has many different surfaces for the light to play on. These include a cylinder (the can), a cone (the flute coming up to the spout), a convex oval (the end of the spout), and the flat surface of the handles.

After penciling in the flowers, begin putting in the shadows where they will be darkest, based on the light source which is directly above the can.

5 Finish drawing in the flowers next so that you can begin to add the shading.

Clean up unwanted lines around the flowers with an eraser.

As we begin the final shading, pay attention to the direction of your pencil marks. Follow the contour of the surface you are drawing using the crosshatching technique.

97

When you are done, your drawing should look something like this. Don't worry if some of the lines are not exactly where you want them or if the shadows are a little off. You can imagine that the watering can is "broken in" after years of service.

Jesus answered, "Everyone who drinks this water will be thirsty again, but whoever drinks the water I give him will never thirst.

Indeed, the water I give him will become in him a spring of water welling up to eternal life."

— John 4:13-14

"The Watered Lilies"

The Master stood in His garden,
Among the lilies fair,
Which His own right hand had planted,
And trained with tend'rest care.

He looked at their snowy blossoms,
And marked with observant eye
That the flowers were sadly drooping,
For their leaves were parched and dry.

"My lilies need to be watered,"
The Heavenly Master said;
"Wherein shall I draw it for them,
And raise each drooping head?"

Close to His feet on the pathway,
Empty, and frail, and small,
An earthen vessel was lying,
Which seemed no use at all;

But the Master saw, and raised it
From the dust in which it lay,
And smiled, as He gently whispered,
"This shall do My work today."

"It is but an 'earthen' vessel,
But it lay so close to Me;
It is small, but it is empty—
That is all it needs to be."

So to the fountain He took it,
And filled it full to the brim;
How glad was the earthen vessel
To be of some use to Him!

He poured forth the living water
Over His lilies fair,
Until the vessel was empty,
And again He filled it there.

He watered the drooping lilies
Until they revived again;
And the Master saw with pleasure.
That His labor had not been vain.

His own hand had drawn the water
Which refreshed the thirsty flowers;
But He used the earthen vessel
To convey the living showers.

And to itself it whispered,
As He laid it aside once more,
"Still will I lie in His pathway,
Just where I did before.

"Close would I keep to the Master,
Empty would I remain,
And perhaps some day He may use me
To water His flowers again."

—Anonymous

Drawing: Garden Tools
Lesson: Tending with Diligence

All hard work brings a profit, but mere talk leads only to poverty.
—Proverbs 14:23

Beautiful gardens that are full of fragrant flower beds and luscious, healthy fruit trees don't just happen by wishing alone—there is hard work involved! The same is true for your heart's "garden." Tending the garden of your soul is a combined work between you and the Master Gardener. He provides the "inspiration" through the power of His Holy Spirit, and you provide the "perspiration" through your diligence to tend to the garden of your soul through regular times of Bible study, prayer, and fellowship with others. If you are faithful to weed out bad thoughts and behavior daily, and to nurture and care for the tender plants of godliness in your garden—such as love, peace, and self-control—you will get the wonderful result of gorgeous "roses"!

1 This lesson is about tending with diligence, and this drawing is going to require that you use those skills. You'll need to take your time, pay attention to the details, and then stick with it.

As always, start with blocking out the shapes, as I've done here.

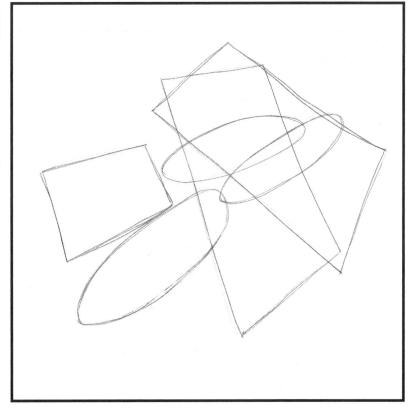

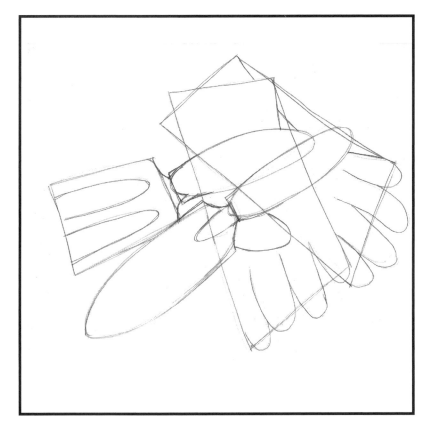

2 Next, begin to define the main characteristics of the drawing by laying out the fingers of the gloves, the fork of the cultivator, and the shape of the trowel.

Try to use a series of short, fast lines to get the shapes looking smooth. Start out lightly until you get the lines that you want. Look closely at the trowel blade and you'll see many lines that end up building that shape. Once your lines are where you want them, you can go in with a darker line that looks straight. Finally, remove the guidelines with careful erasing.

3 Define the shapes by drawing in heavier lines. Because man-made objects need to be carefully drawn to show the precise, machined way they are made, you'll need to take your time as you do the trowel and cultivator. The gloves are a little less exacting at this stage of the drawing.

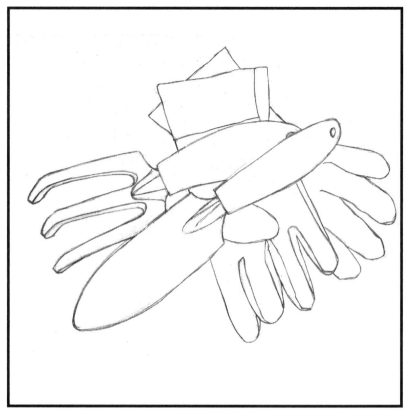

4 Start working in the shadows. In this case, you'll do something a little different. You will use shading as usual to indicate the light source, but you will also use shading to frame the drawing. Don't forget to leave the highlighted area white.

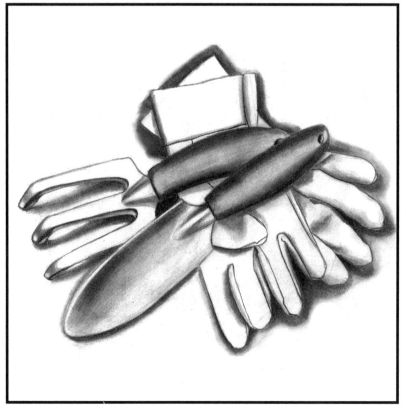

You'll see by the way the shadows are coming off of the forks of the cultivator, and where the light is on the scoop of the trowel, that I've placed the light source above, behind, and to the left of the subject. So why is there shading all around the cuffs of the gloves? We do that to frame our drawing and to help us define the edges of lighter objects.

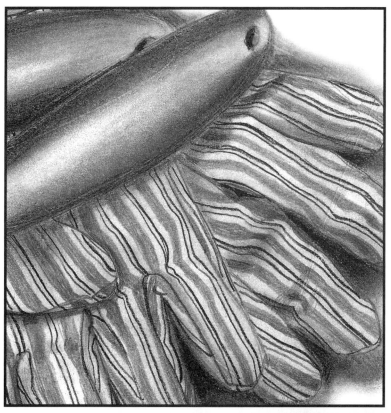

5 It is time to sharpen your pencil and begin to work the details. The thing that really makes this drawing special is the pattern of the fabric. While it may look hard at first, it's really not as difficult as it is time consuming. Just sit back, relax, and have fun with it.

Try to imagine the lumpy, wavy texture of the thick fabric, and draw a line that follows that shape. Make sure you evenly space the lines apart. When you are done, make the rest of the lines in that finger follow that same path, and you'll be amazed at how quickly it starts to look great!

Feel free to be your own glove designer and alter the pattern according to your choice (polka dots, flowers, or even leave them plain).

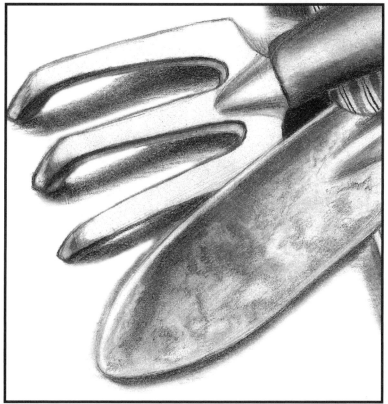

6 While the trowel and the cultivator are both made of metal, they are worn in different ways based on the kind of work they do.

The trowel has been roughed up over the years from digging past rocks and pebbles. The cultivator loosens up already turned soil. Because of this difference in usage, the shading to show texture is different. The cultivator needs to be clean and smooth, while the trowel needs a mottled, uneven, scuffed-up style of shading. To achieve the texture on the trowel, use the scribbling technique.

7 If you are like I am, it has probably taken you awhile to get to this step. But with a few more touches you'll be finished. Go in with a darker pencil and build up the deepest shadows under the tools and the gloves to make them stand out. Define the lines around the fingers of the gloves. If you need to, use your eraser to lighten up the highlights. When you are done, your picture might look something like this.

As you look at these tools for building a garden, remember that God has also given you tools for tending your spiritual garden. I pray that you take the tools God has given you and diligently tend the garden of your heart. Make it a place that you and God will enjoy forever and ever.

Amen.

"Results and Roses"

The man who wants a garden fair,
Or small or very big,
With flowers growing here and there,
Must bend his back and dig.

The things are mighty few on earth
That wishes can attain.
Whate'er we want of any worth
We've got to work to gain.

It matters not what goal you seek
Its secret here reposes:
You've got to dig from week to week
To get Results or Roses.

–Edgar A. Guest (1881-1959)

THE BEST THINGS IN LIFE ARE NEAREST:
BREATH IN YOUR NOSTRILS,
LIGHT IN YOUR EYES,

FLOWERS AT YOUR FEET,
DUTIES AT YOUR HAND,
THE PATH OF RIGHT JUST BEFORE YOU.

THEN DO NOT GRASP AT THE STARS,
BUT DO LIFE'S PLAIN,
COMMON WORK AS IT COMES,

CERTAIN THAT DAILY DUTIES AND DAILY
BREAD ARE THE SWEETEST THINGS IN LIFE.

—ROBERT LOUIS STEVENSON (1850-1894)

THE HIGHEST REWARD FOR A PERSON'S TOIL
IS NOT WHAT THEY GET FOR IT, BUT WHAT
THEY BECOME BY IT.

—JOHN RUSKIN (1819-1900)

"The Gentle Gardener"

I'd like to leave but daffodills
to mark my little way,
To leave but tulips red and white
behind me as I stray;
I'd like to pass away from earth
and feel I'd left behind
But roses and forget-me-nots
for all who come to find.
I'd like to sow the barren spots
with all the flowers of earth,
To leave a path where those who come
should find but gentle mirth;
And when at last I'm called upon
to join the heavenly throng
I'd like to feel along my way
I'd left no sign of wrong.
And yet the cares are many
and the hours of toil are few;
There is not time enough on earth
for all I'd like to do;
But, having lived and having toiled,
I'd like the world to find
Some little touch of beauty
that my soul had left behind.

–Edgar A. Guest (1881-1959)

HE WHO WORKS HIS LAND WILL HAVE
ABUNDANT FOOD.
—PROVERBS 12:11

The Greatest Plan on Earth: The Plan of Salvation

God desired for you to be His child even before He created the earth. That is why you were created—to be God's child. Ephesians 1:4-5 says, "In love he predestined us to be adopted as his sons through Jesus Christ, in accordance with his pleasure and will." First John 3:1 says, "How great is the love the Father has lavished on us, that we should be called children of God!"

God gives His children the freedom to make choices (free will). He doesn't want a bunch of "robots" programmed to love Him. He wants us to choose to love Him. But our free will can be a problem. When God created Adam and Eve, He allowed them the choice of whether to obey Him or not. They chose not to obey, and mankind has been stuck with this rebellious nature ever since. "For all have sinned and fall short of the glory of God" (Romans 3:23). A rebellious nature causes us to sin, and sin separates us from God, because God Himself is completely sinless. Sin leads to death: "For the wages of sin is death, but the gift of God is eternal life in Christ Jesus our Lord" (Romans 6:23).

God understood our sin problem. He knew that we were unable to get rid of our rebellious nature on our own. Because He is the most perfect, loving Father, He did for us what we could not do for ourselves. He sent His flawless Son, Jesus Christ, to pay the penalty for our sins. Jesus came to earth as a sinless man and took upon Himself our sin nature as He died on a Cross. Our sinful nature died with Him on that Cross. Three days later, Jesus arose from the dead, powerful and victorious! Here's the really good news! "If we have been united with him [Christ] like this in his death, we will certainly also be united with him in his resurrection" (Romans 6:5). If we died with Him, then we shall also live with Him. We can now experience the fullness of life, powerful and victorious over sin, as children of God through the resurrected life of Jesus Christ.

To receive the gift of salvation, first admit that you are trapped in this sin nature and that you need Jesus to save you. Take the free will that God has given you and make a choice—the greatest choice you will ever make—to live with and for Christ. Choose to turn from the old, sinful nature, which leads to death, and make Jesus your life. This is called repentance. "Repent, then, and turn to God, so that your sins may be wiped out" (Acts 3:19). Choose to live this way every day. "Count yourselves dead to sin but alive to God in Christ Jesus" (Romans 6:11). Next, believe and receive! "Yet to all who received him, to those who believed in his name, he gave the right to become children of God—children born not of natural descent, nor of human decision or a husband's will, but born of God" (John 1:12-13). By faith we must trust Jesus and receive Him as our Savior and Lord. It's that simple.

Now that you are a child of God Almighty, Creator of Heaven and Earth, you have an incredible inheritance:

1. You have eternal life with Christ now and forever (John 3:16).

2. Your sins are forgiven (Colossians 1:13-14).

3. You are holy and righteous through the blood of Jesus. When God sees you, He sees you through the life of His perfect Son (Philippians 3:9).

4. You now have Christ's life living in you through the Holy Spirit, who is your Helper sent from God (John 14:16).

5. You can be assured of your salvation. When Christ died on the Cross, He proclaimed, "It is finished." This means He has done everything necessary for your salvation. You do not need to earn it or work for it. You only have to believe and let Christ live His life in you (Ephesians 2:8-9). By faith you have received this wonderful new life in Christ. Now by faith, let His life live through you!

Here are some simple steps to do once you have accepted Christ into your heart:

- Tell someone else (preferably another Christian) about the commitment you just made to the Lord.
- Find a church that teaches the Bible and attend it regularly. Get involved in a home Bible study group.
- Get water baptized. Talk to your pastor and parents about this.
- Seek out other Christians in your school or in other places and develop new friendships.

Enjoy your relationship with Jesus—your very closest Forever Friend!

Grow your faith with Violet's other garden-themed companion products!

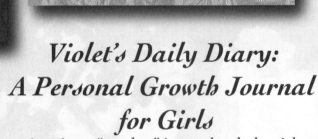

Violet's Life Lessons: Growing Toward God
An in-depth garden-themed study guide to help girls grow in their relationship with Christ.

ISBN 978-1-928749-62-2

Violet's Daily Diary: A Personal Growth Journal for Girls
A unique "garden" journal to help girls chart the climate, growth, and progress of their heart's "garden."

ISBN 978-1-928749-61-5

They work together to help you cultivate a thriving faith in God!

Collect all of our Violet products!

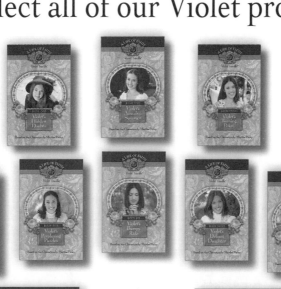

Check out our web site at www.alifeoffaith.com!

- Find out about all the *A Life of Faith* role models
- Get news about the time periods they lived in
- Learn to live a life of faith like them
- Find out about *A Life of Faith* products
- Explore page after page of inspiring advice to help you grow in your relationship with God!

Ordinary Girls • Extraordinary Faith

A LIFE OF FAITH®

Girls Club

An Imaginative New Approach
to Faith Education

*I*magine…an easy way to gather the young girls in your community for fun, fellowship, and faith-inspiring lessons that will further their personal relationship with our Lord, Jesus Christ. Now you can, simply by hosting an A Life of Faith Girls Club.

This popular Girls Club was created to teach girls to live a *lifestyle* of faith.

Through the captivating, Christ-centered, historical fiction stories of Elsie Dinsmore, Millie Keith, Violet Travilla, and Laylie Colbert, each Club member will come to understand God's love for her, and will learn how to deal with timeless issues all girls face, such  as bearing rejection, resisting temptation, overcoming fear, forgiving when it hurts, standing up for what's right, etc. The fun-filled Club meetings include skits and dramas, application-oriented discussion, themed crafts and snacks, fellowship and prayer. What's more, the Club has everything from official membership cards to a Club Motto and original Theme Song!

For more info about our Girls Clubs, call or log on to:
www.alifeoffaith.com • **1-800-840-2641**